SELF-CRITICISM AFTER THE DEFEAT

Sadik al-Azm

SELF-CRITICISM
AFTER THE DEFEAT

*Translated from the Arabic
by George Stergios*

SAQI

ISBN 978-0-86356-488-8

First published 1968 by Dar al-Tali'ah [Vanguard Press]
Printing and Publication, Beirut

This first English edition published 2011 by Saqi Books

A full CIP record for this book is available from the British Library.
A full CIP record for this book is available from the Library of Congress.

Printed and bound by CPI Group (UK) Ltd, Croydon, CRO 4YY

SAQI
26 Westbourne Grove, London W2 5RH
www.saqibooks.com

CONTENTS

A Book and Its Truth:
Sadik al-Azm's *Self-Criticism after the Defeat*

FOUAD AJAMI

At the remove of some four decades, I still recall the startling surprise with which I read Sadik al-Azm's *Self-Criticism after the Defeat*. I was in my early twenties, the Six Day War of June 5 1967, was then a year old. My generation had not fully taken in the defeat of the Arab armies in that war. We had come into our own in the aftermath of the Suez War, we had been told that a new Arab world had arisen, and that the Egyptian Gamal Abdel Nasser had conceived a world free of the old doubts and compromises and weaknesses. We had hung on the man's words: the Beirut of my boyhood – at least the Muslim part of it – was Nasser's, as were, it is easy to recall, vast swaths of the Arab world. The defeat served a notice on all that: Arab political life would never be the same.

Yet for all the enormity of that defeat – the loss of the Golan Heights, and the West Bank and Gaza, the flight of the Egyptian army, the shame that attended the defeat in a culture of pride – young Arabs didn't have the language and the intellectual equipment to describe what had befallen their world. We had abandoned God and God abandoned us, said what we would later come to describe as the Islamists. We had assaulted the proper order of things – property and hierarchy and tradition – said the monarchists and the traditionalists: we had filled the earth with sedition, and had reaped the whirlwind. A liberal or two said that the Arabs needed a scientific culture and modern armies – as though those could be bought off the rack, as though their absence said nothing about the contemporary condition of the Arabs.

It was into that great confusion that Sadik al-Azm, an American-educated philosopher of Syrian birth then teaching at the American University of Beirut, published his seminal book. Everything about *Self-Criticism after the Defeat* announced that a new age of Arabic letters and Arabic writing had begun. The book was brief and una-dorned when the Arabic writing had hitherto been ponderous and flowery. There was truth in the book, and candor, a coura-geous man taking on the pieties and the beliefs of that era. Sadik al-Azm belonged to a bigger world than the Beirut and Damascus of his time. He was highly educated (a Ph.D. in philosophy from Yale), he was widely read, he saw the Arab defeat for what it was: an indictment of Arab culture, a verdict on the sort of world that the military officers and the revolutionaries of the era had built. For the preceding decade, Arabs had fought a sterile ideological battle – the American political scientist Malcolm Kerr had dubbed it the Arab Cold War that pitted the monarchies in Jordan, the Arabian Peninsula, and the Gulf against Gamal Abdel Nasser and his generation.

Al-Azm was a political heretic: he saw no great discontinuity between the Old Order that had lost the battle for Palestine in 1948 and the New Men who lost this new war two decades later. Little had changed in the intervening years, he wrote. The New Men had been a colossal failure, and al-Azm called upon the Arabs, on the seventh day of this Six Day War (to use the language of the Israeli writer Meron Benvenisti) to see their world for what it was. He was a man without illusions: I don't think he saw the onset of a revolution that would remake Arab culture. True, he began his book with a powerful precedent: the defeat of Tsarist Russia at the hands of Japan in 1904–1905. He saw, and worked with a historical analogy: a big, traditional empire, steeped in superstition and tyranny, defeated by a smaller, more modern power. Like the Russians who thought that they would push those "impudent Asiatics" into the sea, the crowds in the Arab world had been sure of victory. These were "Zionist gangs" on the battlefield, it was said. No one had prepared that "Arab street" for the possibility of defeat: the armies were big, bloated institutions, and the hero-leader, Gamal Abdel Nasser, cast his spell over the crowd. There was no reason, no sober analysis, amid the crowd, only passion and belief. No one had told ordinary Arabs that Israel was there to stay, that she had won the struggle for statehood on her own, that the verdict of the 1948 war could not be reversed. A Moroccan historian, Abdullah Laroui, poignantly depicts the popular Arab attitude on this great question: "on a certain day everything would be obliterated and instantaneously reconstructed and the new inhabitants would leave, as if by magic, the land that they have despoiled; in this way will justice be dispensed to the victims, on that day when the presence of God shall again make itself felt."

God had failed the Arabs on June 5th, and political magic had failed them as well. This was a captive population for all practical purposes, the world beyond was in on the magnitude of the Arab defeat, but the vast majority of Arabs had turned away from the verdict of the war. On June 9th, Nasser submitted his resignation, but the believers would have none of that. They held onto their wounded hero, and Sadik al-Azm saw nothing here similar to the self-criticism and upheaval that had hit Russia in 1905. Al-Azm was writing in the immediate aftermath of the Arab defeat. By the Russian calendar, it had taken a dozen years before the autocracy had been brought down: the external forms of Russian life were emptied of meaning. Al-Azm couldn't be sure if the dominant order of Arab power would hold. He and others of his outlook, intellectuals and writers stung by the military defeat, were now given to the belief that the word could perhaps remake the political world. Beirut was the home of this breed of young intellectuals, and al-Azm (of aristocratic Damascene family – the al-Azms were one of the great families of Syria's land-owning aristocracy) was to emerge as perhaps his generation's most influential public intellectual. Nothing was beyond the scrutiny of this band of writers. The official world had been exposed, the pamphleteers and the writers were on their own, and the armed men were soon to follow – the Palestinian fighters, the *fedayeen*, who became the other symbol of this time of tumult in the life of the Arabs.

It was easy at the time to exaggerate the weakness of the dominant order – the monarchs in Jordan and the Arabian Peninsula, the military regimes in Cairo, Damascus, and Baghdad. The order seemed, on the face of it, ripe for the plucking. The men who shaped public discourse could be forgiven the thought that the whole big edifice of the ruling order could be toppled. The men in the saddle were willing to bide their time. This revolutionary moment, the military autocrats and the dynasties reasoned, was destined to pass. Six years after the defeat of 1967, the dominant order would mount its rear-guard action: the October War of 1973. New oil wealth would come to the Arabs, and a legend could be offered ordinary men and women that a new era of Arab power beckoned. But men are never given the gift of prophecy: the intervening years between those two wars spawned expectations of imminent change.

Above all, in *Self-Criticism* and other equally daring works to come, al-Azm sought to strip Arab thought of its belief in fate and folk tales and superstition. In Cairo, a legend had erupted that the Virgin Mary had made an appearance in one of the city's neighborhoods, that she had come to console the Egyptians in their hour of adversity: a writer out to assert the primacy of rationalist thinking, cause-and-effect, and the world as it is had his work cut out for him. It was Sadik al-Azm's gift that he relished the fight. What he most wanted, what gave his book its power, was the theme of responsibility. The regime in Cairo had taken the plunge into a war for which it hadn't been prepared. Yet, Cairo's tribunes never accepted the burden of the choices they made. The leading proponent of Nasserism was then the journalist Mohamed Heikal, editor of the powerful daily *Al-Ahram*. He had shaped the debate of the preceding decade, he had been glib and self-confident, he wrote in a knowing, accessible style, the glibness concealing the liberties Heikal took with evidence, with causation itself, the conspiracy theories he peddled to an audience taken in by his storytelling. (I know from whence I speak, even in my teens I had been a devotee of his columns: I awaited them with eagerness as they appeared every Friday in *Al-Ahram*.) Heikal had misled two generations of Arabs; with Sadik al-Azm's critique Heikal was to undergo fierce scrutiny. A new generation of truth-tellers had found its voice. The reader of al-Azm's book will see the clash of two outlooks, a culture of concealment and double-speak and evasion coming face to face with relentless rationalism.

There was moralism in the way the Arabs had described and

spoken of their defeat: Israel had struck first, they sermonized, she had resorted to "deceit and surprise," and the Arab armies had been victims of a premeditated aggression. Al-Azm would have none of this: the Arabs had themselves to blame, they had insisted that they were at war with Israel and that the battle of liberation was not far. A "traditional people" who spoke of war in obsolete terms of chivalry and the "clinking of swords," the Arabs were not ready for a modern war, they had thought of the war as a triumphant "excursion." To this new war, al-Azm writes, the Arabs brought traditional notions of sexual honor. The refugees who fled before Israeli armor said that they emerged with their "honor" intact to protect the women from sexual violation. This was then (and remains) a prudish society, the taboo on a discussion of sexual mores and sisters and wives and mothers strictly observed. I still recall the controversy stirred by that discussion: the men who "fled with their honor" handed their enemy a land "empty of inhabitants," Al-Azm wrote. The war had exposed a society's inadequacy in the modern world; the Arabs had not yet entered the age of modern citizenship. They fought, and fled, as tribes; they sheltered their families as best they could, but cared little for the public domain. They lived in the idle hope that someday their numbers, their moral claim, the justness of their cause, would settle this great struggle in their favor. They consoled themselves with the legend that whenever they engaged their enemy "face to face," they had fought and died bravely. Modern war, of course, paid no heed to such notions of chivalry. A tradition-bound society had gone to war, and the war had simply exposed its inadequacy. The "human element," as Nasser himself now admitted, had been deficient. There was a lack of fit between the modern weapons and the Arab soldiers who used these weapons. And there were the superstitions of earlier ages which had survived the surface modernization of the 1950s and 1960s – the belief that the angels who had fought on the side of the Prophet Mohammed would descend and take part in this war. Al-Azm had pity for the Arabs of his time, he had for them the gift of his clarity. They were his people, his dissent a true act of fidelity.

Nowadays, we speak, and rightly so, of the cultural isolation of the Arabs – the fact, for example, that a vast Arab world translates into Arabic only a fifth of the number of books that Greece, with

its eleven million people, translates into Greek. But we have eth-
nocentrisms of our own, in this big and open American republic.
It is a wonder that this seminal book was never translated into
English. The shadow of American power lies across that Greater
Middle East, but the people of that region remain mostly stran-
gers to us, and we ought to do better. We owe a debt of gratitude
to George Stergios for retrieving this unique document, this sin-
gular work in Arabic thought and letters. The translation is fresh
and vibrant, and even at the remove of a good deal of time, Sadik
al-Azm's book remains a stirring document. He told his people the
sort of truths that outsiders are too embarrassed to tell – even when
they were themselves able to see these truths. This Arab culture has
not been kind to those from within its ranks who tell it truths it
does not wish to hear. In the intervening four decades since this
book's publication, Sadik al-Azm was to know both eminence and
persecution: he has been both honored and maligned. He was
tried, in liberal Lebanon no less, for his assault on Islamic religious
dogma. In those years filled with controversy and expectations of
great change in Arab life, the American University of Beirut would
dismiss him from its faculty, and self-professed liberals would walk
away from him. He was to know the dissenter's life in a culture that
asks for uniformity and obedience.

Sadik al-Azm had not foreseen a big breakthrough for the Arab
world, and it was not to come. In a brilliant essay, written for the
Boston Review in 2004, he looked in at the Arabs, for yet another
autopsy, and little had changed. I could do no better than quote his
own haunting words on the stagnation in the world of the Arabs.

A cultural form of schizophrenia is also attendant on the Arab
(and Muslim) world's tortured, protracted, and reluctant adap-
tation to European modernity. This process has truly made the
modern Arabs into the Hamlet of our times, doomed to unre-
lieved tragedy, forever hesitating, procrastinating, and wavering between the old and the new, between *asala* and *mu'asara*
(authenticity and contemporaneity), between *turath* and
tajdid (heritage and renewal), between *huwiyya* and *hadatha*
(identity and modernity), and between religion and secular-
ity, while the conquering Fortinbrases of the world inherit the

new century. No wonder, then, to quote Shakespeare's most famous drama, that "the time is out of joint" for the Arabs and "something is rotten in the state." No wonder as well if they keep wondering whether they are the authors of their woes or whether "there's a divinity that shapes [their] ends."

Spring 2010

PREFACE

An Introduction after a Long Interruption

SADIK AL-AZM

On the many occasions in which conversations took place concerning the defeat of the 5th of June 1967, and concerning its persistent effects and influences in the life of the Arabs, I often heard it said that of the many writings produced in the Arab world after the defeat, under titles dealing with the defeat in almost all of its aspects, only three remain in the collective Arab memory (at least among the educated): Nizar Qabbani's poem *Marginal Notes on the Copybook of the Setback*, Saadallah Wannous' play *A Soirée for the 5th of June*, and my book *Self-Criticism after the Defeat*. I want to add here that during some of these conversations, the Syrians present enthusiastically pointed out to everyone else that all of the mentioned works came out of Syria, that is, they were produced by a Syrian poet, a Syrian dramatist, and a Syrian thinker, acknowledging without hesitation the role that Lebanon and, in particular, Beirut, played in their publication.

Qabbani's poem is widely available to readers in his books of poetry and his poetry collections in constant circulation at bookshops, just as the play of Saadallah is within the reach of all those who want to read it through his works printed and published across the whole Arab world. As for the book *Self-Criticism after the Defeat*, it has remained out-of-print and absent from bookshops for more than a quarter-century, more concretely, since the last conventional

Arab war with Israel, the October War of 1973. After that date, Dar al-Tali'ah [Vanguard Press], the original publisher of the book, let it go out of print, after more than ten consecutive printings between the years of 1968 and 1973 (despite prohibitions and confiscations in many of the Arab states). In addition, there were independent printings that took place in the occupied Palestinian territories.

Thus, I want to offer my sincere thanks and profound gratitude to Dar Mamduh 'Adwan for republishing it, and especially to its animating spirit and owner Mrs. Ilham 'Abdulatif 'Adwan for her plan and initiative in republishing it so that it would take its place beside the other two works with which it appears to be tied together forever in the minds of readers, and so that it is available, like them, in bookshops. Moreover, it is now within reach of the rising generations who know nothing of the great Arab defeat of the twentieth century but the official views produced and distributed by the defeated regimes themselves.

On this occasion, I returned to the book and reread it, and while I found that it had certainly aged, it was not to the extent I had anticipated. As for the final judgment of these matters, it is left to each reader according to his circumstances, convictions, concerns, and education, especially for the generations that are not familiar with the defeat except from what they have heard, read or remember from their childhood. As for my personal evaluation, it can be summarized in my belief that the book can still say some important things to the present generations so that they know, at least, from what battles, events, recent history, and failures derives the present situation in which they live.

Certainly there are some signs of haste and confusion in the text, for I wrote it with great speed and under a frightening collective and personal psychological pressure, not only as a result of the defeat, but also as a result of the almost impossible manner in which it occurred and the awful destructive legacy which this startling abrupt collapse left to our entire generation, the generation of the sixties. What made the situation in which I undertook to compose the book more distressing was my personal realization at the time that the state of miserable denial and irresponsible and irrational flight that had prevailed instantly over the defeated was similar to the conditions that sometimes afflict the sick, who are then unable to acknowledge their sickness but instead deny the fact of the illness in their behavior, expressions, delusions, and hallucinations because they are unable to bear the reality of the situation.

This condition of denial and flight prompted me to work with an excess of speed (and even haste) to publish my book, with a dogged insistence on using the expression "the defeat" in order to describe what happened instead of the expression "the setback," which had entered popular, intellectual, and official circulation in order to camouflage what occurred. In fact, the book *Self-Criticism after the Defeat* was the first widely-circulated work that called the defeat by its name publicly and clearly, without any attempt to hide or dilute the effect of the fire and napalm on its victims.

One of the shocking signs of this state of denial was that one of the most prominent leaders of the Arab Nationalist Movement in Lebanon, Muhsin Ibrahim, who was also one of the most important theoreticians of Nasserism and defenders of the Nasserite course in the Arab world, published an article in the Beirut magazine *Al-Hurriya* right after the defeat carrying the self-explanatory title "No, Abdul Nasser Did Not Err and the Arabs Were Not Defeated" (June 14, 1967).

As for Damascus, the slogan circulating with alarming frequency officially and popularly days before the defeat read: "They Will Not Cross." The same slogan continued to circulate for an extended period after they crossed, the matter ended, and the party was over. In Cairo, the Virgin Mary appeared suddenly in a church bearing her name in the suburb of Zeitoun, and the Egyptian mass media (at their head, the dignified newspaper *Al-Ahram*) whipped this appearance almost into a hysteria, eagerly spreading its miraculous, defeat-denying meaning. (I handled the issue of the appearance of the Virgin in fullness in my book *Critique of Religious Thought*.) Everyone who lived through this dark and wretched period certainly remembers how we heard repeated day and night that the "setback" failed to achieve its goals because the progressive Arab regimes did not fall and because the Arab fighter pilots, especially in Egypt, were not harmed in the war and thus were ready to pay back the Israeli enemy twofold as soon as the Soviet Union provided us with new planes to take the place of those we lost in the first moments of the defeat.

In May 1967, President Gamal Abdel Nasser ordered the Egyptian Army to concentrate all its forces and arms in the Sinai and along the border with Israel, despite the fact that much of his army was in Yemen helping the young republic carry on and endure. This move set off an ascending Arab-Israeli military-political dynamic that reached its decisive climax in the morning of Monday the 5th of June. However, before this day it had appeared to everyone on the Arab side as if the awaited moment of the liberation of Palestine had arrived (in the way the Mahdi is awaited). Consequently, a vast wave of psychological mobilization and frighteningly optimistic emotion flooded the Arab world, with every high hope and triumphalist expectation escaping from every leash and at every level: popular, official, military, administrative, academic, intellectual, student, etc.

I remember that on the morning the war broke out I was awoken early by a telephone call in my home in Beirut. I found Adonis on the other end of the line contacting me in order to let me know that the war had begun, Israeli planes were falling one after the other, and the Arab armies were advancing according to the Arab media (via radio broadcasts and transistor radios in those days) and the official military communiqués. We spoke about the war with confidence and without great anxiety since the thought of defeat did not cross the mind of anyone, as if the possibility of Arab defeat was inconceivable. The worst that could happen did not surpass, in our defective and deceived imaginations, a kind of tight draw or new equilibrium between the Israelis and us.

It is impossible to compare the condition of optimistic emotional mobilization, alarming enthusiasm, and wild triumphalist intoxication that prevailed in the Arab world (it touched all of us with its deceptive magic) in the period between the deploying of the Egyptian forces in the Sinai and the moment the war broke out to anything except the similar condition that prevailed in our Arab world the day President Gamal Abdel Nasser announced the nationalization of the Suez Canal in the summer of 1956 and during the momentous events that followed. I do not believe that anyone from this generation truly recovered from this sudden fall from the dizzying heights to the bottom of the abyss of the crushing defeat, which took no more than a few moments.

During this period of mobilization and waiting for war I was discussing the current events with friends, colleagues, acquaintances, activists, and thinkers in Beirut and Damascus in order to try to come to a balanced and rational assessment of what was taking place in the military, political, and international arenas, all of which were replete with apparent maneuvers, distortions, and deceptions. We were following the number of tanks that we possessed and the enemy possessed. We were comparing the respective number of fighter and non-fighter planes. We were tracking the number of troops mobilized on each side of the border, finding out in the final days before the outbreak of the war that Israel had mobilized an army on its border that surpassed in number the sum of Egyptian, Syrian, and Jordanian troops mobilized to enter the battle for the liberation of Palestine. All of our information sources were Western despite their prohibition in every Arab country but Lebanon. Although we did not fully trust them back then, they were the sole available sources except for trickles of information coming from the Soviet Union and some European socialist countries transmitted to us through those same Western media.

I remember that I arrived with some friends in Beirut and Damascus at a scenario concerning the war and its likely course and consequences, relying on a recent precedent that we had witnessed and followed, the grinding war that broke out between Pakistan and India in 1965, at a time in which Pakistan was still united as one country with East Bengal. The scenario that we thought likely to be realized was very conservative in comparison with the surrounding scenarios of immediate triumph proposed with an enthusiasm that swept away everything in its way with an incomparable, explosive emotion.

In accordance with the precedent of the India-Pakistan war, our scenario proposed that the Arab-Israeli war would break out soon, and that after the conflicting armies undertook the destruction of each other's tanks, planes, and weapons, leveled some of each other's vital installations, and killed, ejected, and imprisoned the greatest number possible of each other's armies, the great powers would intervene forcefully, especially the United States and the Soviet Union, by means of the United Nations and the Security Council. They would arrange the announcement of a ceasefire followed by military withdrawals to the previous borders and then proceed to final arrangements of a kind that we had witnessed in the India-Pakistan war, where the traditional balance between the two countries was restored, with Pakistan bearing a relatively greater loss as a result of the war.

Although this scenario appeared to me very realistic, reasonable, and likely, any expression of it or of expectations that included it in the feverishly optimistic atmosphere prevailing among the Arabs just before the 5th of June would be immediately suspected of defeatism, negativism, and pessimism, even within private gatherings and closed circles of discussion. No one would dare to express it or something similar publicly since that would discount the possibility of Israel's ignominious defeat and the inevitability of the liberation of Palestine, at least for the present time.

After the 5th of June, the same scenario appears like a summer night's dream in its rosiness, optimism, unreality, and irrationality compared to what really happened. I leave to the reader the task of reaching the conclusions he finds appropriate and deriving the lesson that he finds valuable after reading the book.

Beirut, March 2007

INTRODUCTION

The Persistence of the Defeat /
The Persistence of the Critical Book

FAISAL DARRAJ

Forty years ago, the Arab world lived through its great defeat of the twentieth century, a defeat that resumed, in different circumstances, the defeat of Muhammad Ali Pasha in the nineteenth century. Sadik al-Azm, in his book *Self-Criticism after the Defeat*, wanted to analyze the causes of the defeat and suggest, theoretically, how to undo it, before he recognized that it, like many others, was a homegrown defeat, that it did not have its source in "external conspiracies" but in persistent Arab impotence, distributed equally among the people and the authorities. This homegrown defeat, which adds to the rest of the defeats a new defeat, is what maintains the currency of Dr. al-Azm's book, even if the transformations of the defeat into a "natural phenomenon" raise other issues.

This book, which pondered the defeat of the 5th of June in 1967, encompasses three testimonies. The first is that of the nobility of critical thought and its estrangement. The second is that of the Arab social structure dominated by a swamp-like stagnation. The third is that of the outcome of the question of Palestine, once known as "the greatest Arab cause." Whether these three testimonies are complete or incomplete, they indicate a lamentable Arab situation that the Egyptian economist Dr. Fawzy Mansour years ago gave the sharply defined epithet: "the exit of the Arabs from history."

Sadik al-Azm belongs to the few Arab intellects who transform culture into a critical intervention, treating living national and social issues, far from the scholastic abstractions and even further from the "delusions of authenticity" and "virtues of particularism." For he realizes that the Arab world, like it or not, lives in a universal time, and that this universal time compares the achievements of one people and another, without regard to "ancient glories," real or imagined. The critical comparison that the "Bildungs-philosopher" practices depends on a demonstrative reason relying on a comparative approach, an approach that affirms that the value of a given society is measured against the value of another, because human societies are not found in isolation. This conception, which does not halt much before Zionist racism and the deadly Israeli war machine, because it takes these for granted, is what prods the critical mind to compare a modern colonialist society and an Arab society "intending liberation," content in imitation and the reproduction of traditions. Relying on the principles of critical reason, Sadik al-Azm pondered the causes of the June defeat and criticized, subsequently, the "theory and practice" of the Palestinian resistance, dealt with "the Sadat period," gave his view on the relation of religious belief to narrative fiction, and undertook as many polemics and dialogues as possible. He was in what he did, right or wrong, clear, consistent, incapable of stammering or "theoretical courtesies," never changing his positions with the seasons. He wanted to be a modern intellectual in his political-theoretical contributions, connecting academic knowledge and the questions of life, and to look at different societal horizons, replacing the old with the new, and confronting the tyranny of inherited habits with the awakening of the rejuvenated mind. He practiced his criticism as a free agent, rejecting the rationalization of the deadly defeats in the name of futuristic slogans, and rejecting even more the placing of human responsibility beyond man, for the future is a product of human behavior in the present. Indeed, the lived present is the sole "essential" time, for it is what the past arrives at and it is what the future is formed in. He revealed in his free critical practice the intimate relationship between reason and freedom, because reason is formed in the freedom to accept, reject, and test, thus moving from what it knows to what it does not know. This kind of reason stands at a wide distance from an inert static reason that Sadik al-Azm broke with completely. Although this calcified, absolutist reason, which is content with custom and sanctifies it, is able to shower al-Azm with charges of insolence, heresy, and trifling with what should not be the subject of trifling, still the apparent proof for what he said exists to a scandalous degree in a debilitated Arab reality, reproducing its misery and achieving what is called today "the Arab exception," that is, the singularity of Arab society in rejecting the bases of democratic life. The fact of the matter is that this singularity which should be rejected by sound human sense is what makes of every Arab battle a defeat, and guarantees the next defeat.

In the beginning of the twentieth century, in 1906, to be precise, Najib Azuri published a book (in French) that enjoyed some measure of fame, its title being *The Awakening of the Arab Nation*. The author, who was an active journalist, attributed the shabbiness of the Arab situation to Ottoman rule, believing that the liberation from this rule would be the entry into a new golden age, restoring the nation to its past glory, and permitting it to deliver a firm sweeping defeat to the coming infernal project: the Zionist project. The Ottomans departed and the Arab situation deteriorated further, until Constantin Zureiq arrived in the fifth decade of the last century and composed his book *Of Nationalist Thought*, considering the proper horizon for the Arab world to be in a crystallized Arab national project. When Palestine fell in 1948, Arab fragmentation and the "colluding regimes" took the blame, and were quickly overthrown by a popular movement, which brought regimes that promised the elimination of backwardness and fragmentation, and made the reclaiming of Palestine "the great Arab cause everywhere." As for the great test of "the essence of Arabism," it came with the June defeat, which gave to "the great cause" in its subsequent declining states the following succession of names: "the Imperialist-Arab struggle," "the Arab-Zionist struggle," "the Arab-Israeli struggle," "the Palestine-Israel struggle," arriving finally at the Oslo Agreement that reduced "historical Palestine" to a collection of contiguous small prisons. Two things are clear in all of this: the renewal of the defeats under different social-authoritarian conditions, and the reproduction of the relations of backwardness in a renewed form, which allows for serial defeats that "expel the Arabs from history."

Sadik al-Azm criticized, in his book *Self-Criticism after the Defeat*, the Arab social structure invariable in its defeats: for it was defeated in the Ottoman period, and it was defeated in the period preceding independence, and it was defeated again in the period of the "independent states." Obviously, it is the folly of follies for the intellect to derive the defeat from the "Arab essence," and to derive this essence from an eternally defeated character, for this makes of victory and defeat an impossible question, and it makes criticism something superfluous and unnecessary. Nevertheless, the search for ways to contain the defeat requires its clear acknowledgment, without eloquence or deceit, for whoever wants to know something must know it by its name. Perhaps the confronting of deceit with truth, that is, the clear acknowledgment of the phenomenon, since defeat is defeat and victory is victory, is the primary virtue of Sadik al-Azm's book, which anchored clear criticism on a conception that does not separate words from their objects.

Al-Azm treated the negative aspects immanent in a backward society using a particular language, i.e., he treated the unity of theoretical and practical ideology, in the societal sense of the term, using a different kind of language. He approached, in a polemical style, five basic aspects: 1) ignorance concerning oneself and others, or ignorance of the facts concerning all the sides that were once involved in the battle between the "reactionary" and the "progressive" forces; 2) rationalization that shifts the facts from their true places to illusory places, which clears "the Arabs" from responsibility and considers the defeat as an "unethical phenomenon" directed by forces far removed from the "Arab virtues"; 3) fabrication that scatters realities and neglects to reconnect them, such as those who separate the causes of the defeat from the practices of the ruling authorities, or say that modern battle can be understood through standards alien to modern times, or look for an impossible equation that derives modern technology from "Arab chivalry"; 4) a revived "fatalism" that dissolves daily facts into the dualities of faith versus apostasy, the right path versus the wrong path, and virtue versus vice, as if the "enemies of Islam" triumph over their enemies by faith alone; and 5) finally arriving at "the non-existent citizen," who blots out the national interest with familial, tribal, and sectarian interests, transforming the homeland into a neutral place, defined only by opposing interests.

Sadik al-Azm wanted, when he analyzed the negative manifestations after the June defeat, to analyze the social phenomena that led ineluctably to the defeat before June and after it. Al-Azm analyzed, in this sense, backwardness as such, before Mahdi Amil analyzed the authoritarian policies that guarantee the conditions for "the growth of backwardness" and suggest the bases for "the science of the renewal of the defeat." For it is the reigning political authority in the Arab world that has monopolized since the birth of the "independent states" the "national decision," thus turning society into an elongated, useless appendix. The proper question is the following: What makes Arab intellectuals, from Najib Azuri to Taha Hussein and from Constantin Zureiq to Yasin al-Hafiz and from Mahdi Amil to Fawzi Mansour and Saadallah Wannous confront a society that firmly combines defeat and backwardness?

In his book, Sadik al-Azm criticized different ideas, distributed among the right and left that indicate, up to a point, an almost homogenous Arab thinking, which allows the abstract to dominate the concrete, and turns the activity of changing reality to an impoverished mental process. Although political authority did not play the role for him that it did, subsequently, with Mahdi Amil, al-Azm broaches it in the discussion of topics such as production, pedagogical policies, and the presumed unity of theory and practice. The fact of the matter is that al-Azm, being a liberal Marxist, did not believe in that formal separation between "the right" and "the left," or in that floating eloquence about "progress" and "progressives," because he was, and still is, defending the possibility of a social modernity that extends to human beings a modern view of the world. For independence in a backward country negates the meaning of independence, just as the backward consciousness undermines the meaning of progressive ideas. This modern perspective, one that rejects the reduction of the battle with Israel to an impoverished utilitarian glossary, made him, when he treated the June defeat, discuss 1) the secular conception of the world that liberates "the fighting mind" from myths, fables, and gratuitous transcendental guarantees, 2) science as a productive social force, 3) the initiating mind that chooses answers adequate to reality, 4) the liberation of women that is the condition of the liberation of society, and 5) national production that is not rational unless it adopts rational standards and a call for a modern culture, individuals who belongs to their free mental possibilities, and a homeland that is not obscured by impoverished organic references. Thus this book can be read at two levels. The first assigns to historical reality causes capable of explanation. The second, deeper, refers to the culture of social modernity, which looks at theory for its practice, at discourse for its effects, at science for its applications, at reason for the language it uses, and sees, therefore, the renewed defeat in the fixed reference point that produces it. Sadik al-Azm's question has been, in his various writings, the following: What are the sources of backwardness, and what are the after-effects produced by backwardness? These are the two questions that Sadik al-Azm has been raising, in a polemical form, for more than forty years.

In his recently published book, *Alienation in Arab Culture*, Dr. Halim Barakat pursued Sadik al-Azm's question in a different context. Al-Azm studied the defeat in a time in which it appeared that it could be transcended, for the regimes had not yet settled into a permanent state of impotence, the public space had not yet fallen into a "faith-based populism" that was anxious about the torments of the grave and that displaced the question of Palestine to the unforeseeable future, and "the philosophy of progress" had not fragmented into a scatter of articulations difficult to unite. Halim Barakat observed the effective course of the defeat ending in two basic propositions. Sadik al-Azm stated the first of them, that the family is the reference point of action and thought defining the norms of the individual and the meaning of the homeland, morals and virtue. The second, unanticipated by al-Azm and everyone else, is the impotence that places historical questions and the Arab response to them in two different distant spaces, as if in different worlds.

Although in the Arab world there is something that creates the illusion of a social movement, that is, of a rebellion against impotence and defeat, this movement is marginal and meager because of the homogeneity of the authoritarian and the "fatalistic populist" view, which differ in content but not in structure. In most situations, the first of the two is oppressive, univocal, and does not acknowledge the other, and the second is dogmatically self-assured, claiming a monopoly on absolute truth. What is absent in both is the lived reality about which Sadik al-Azm speaks. In any case, the defeat produced, in its first stage, a social crisis, which the authorities tried to solve through policies that impoverished and buried society, and that the buried society tried to solve through a "metaphysics of ultimate redemption," which calls for a "rightly-guided period" that will never return or awaits a "blessed solution" which will not come. The fact of the matter is that Sadik al-Azm composed his book in a calamitous time that announced, despite its embarrassment, that it was possible to surpass the crisis. For feeling the crisis was an expression of the existence of life and of the will to defend life. However, Halim Barakat composed his book in the period of the "death of the crisis," that is, the death of society, for there is no Arab authority capable of renewing itself after it has settled into a state of "scandalous exceptionalism," and the "absolute fatalism" that has triumphed at the populist level is not concerned with earthly matters. The final remainder, in both cases, is an "Oriental particularism," which gives to one human side tyranny, corruption, weakness, ignorance, and immiseration, and the other side, democracy, science, technical knowledge, the rule of law, and the rights of citizenship.

If the "liberation of Palestine" is a patriotic-nationalist deed then it must comprise "freedom," and if this deed cannot unfold except within a modern perspective since the Zionist enemy relies on modern instruments, then what remains of the project of the liberation of Palestine in an Arab space that does not accept freedom and does not acknowledge social modernity? Sadik al-Azm touched in his book on the subject of "people's war of liberation," in a language that is incomprehensible in our time, confirming the role of reason, will, and freedom, whose absence turns "a gun" into a "thing" that another "thing" carries. For there is nothing strange in a time in which the kingdom of things is spreading that Palestine almost becomes a Palestinian affair and that the struggle for the sake of Palestine turns into a struggle over "things" big and small, whose first recourse is the "Palestinian Authority." For the Palestinian cause has been reduced to the political authority speaking in the name of Palestine. The struggle between the Palestinian organizations has become a power struggle over the "Authority" while Palestine itself has ended up as a set of battling chimerical "authorities" whose only arbiter is the authority of Israeli superiority. It is entertaining for the Arab reader today to return to the "Arab literature" that followed the fall of Palestine, and to the other literature parallel to it, following the "setback of June," in order to observe the tragic path that transformed the "great Arab cause" into an inessential daily affair closer to banality. The French writer André Malraux said once: "Man is a product of all the things that he has accomplished!"

It could be said that Sadik al-Azm, like Halim Barakat, perhaps, does not discuss the resistance. However, what is this amazing resistance if it is not, in its real meaning, this critical resisting act that strives, up to a point, for an Arab society that respects man: that is the alpha and omega of resistance. In his book, *The Seven Masks of Nasserism*, a book whose objectivity incites admiration, the late Louis Awad discussed the tragedy of Gamal Abdul Nasser, the true nationalist leader, who wanted to liberate Palestine with "shackled soldiers," forgetting, as the writer said, that "prisoners do not fight wars." What Awad said is what Sadik al-Azm said, and what both have said is what Halim Barakat and Constantin Zureiq also said. And Taha Hussein said it before all of them, when he stated in his book, *The Future of Culture in Egypt*, that colonialism is a lesser evil than an independent, backward country. Obviously, these various positions of resistance belong to the space called "culture," that the absence of democracy transforms into alienated actions that each patriotic thinker inherits from a preceding alienated thinker.

The book, *Self-Criticism after the Defeat*, which was published almost forty years ago, still retains its currency today for more than one reason. For the defeat whose causes he delineated continues today, the causes that he subjected to criticism are still with us, and the mentality that justifies what cannot be justified grows actively within. However, the true importance of the book is not in its throwing a beam of light on a historical tragedy that occurred at a specific time, but in the free critical method that explains human disappointment through human reasons, without recourse to fog.

Spring 2007

SELF-CRITICISM
AFTER THE DEFEAT

Sadik al-Azm

A civilization changes when its oppressed element – the humiliation of the slave and the drudgery of the worker – suddenly changes into a value. That is, when the oppressed renounces the attempt to flee from this humiliation in order to seek in it his salvation, and when the worker renounces the attempt to flee from his drudgery in order to find in it the justification for his existence. The factory, which still resembles the church of the catacombs, must become like a cathedral, and man must see in it, instead of the gods, human capacity struggling against the earth.

André Malraux
Man's Fate (1933)

Introduction

I hope that enlightened Arab thinking will have surpassed the stage in which criticism is considered merely the activity of disparagement or the unending enumeration of defects, faults, and shortcomings. In other words, that it will have achieved a stage capable of considering criticism as the precise analysis that identifies weak spots, sources of helplessness, and influences that lead to the presence of these faults and shortcomings. Every criticism undertaken with this understanding is bound to be purposive in its unfolding and positive in its outcome, regardless of how negative and harsh it may appear at first sight. I also hope that the enlightened Arab consciousness will have surpassed the stage preceding the defeat when criticism was always under suspicion, regarded beforehand as an obstacle to proceeding in a revolutionary direction, and as something that strew doubt and weakened Arab military prowess in the face of the challenges of Israel, Zionism, and its colonial backers. For when the Arab military, concerning which no one was allowed to raise doubt, was put to the test, it suffered defeat in a measure that was far beyond the imagination and hopes of its enemies. The best witness to what I have said is what Mohammed Hassanein Heikal stated in one of his articles (*Al-Anwar*, July 12, 1968) concerning how the Soviet leaders reacted to the recent Arab defeat. Heikal says:

> The Soviets were shocked by how the battles that began on the 5th of June turned out. Regardless of what they tried to say about the sources of the failures, they could not accept the magnitude of the defeat for what it was and, with no alternative, began to treat it as if it proceeded from a natural disaster like a hurricane or earthquake.

Even the most skeptical among us never imagined or dreamt that a day would come in which the collapse of the Arab military could be described by analogy with earthquakes, hurricanes, or blind natural disasters.

Readers will find in this investigation a critique and analysis of the states of affairs surrounding and relating to the defeat, as well as a discussion of a number of views and perspectives that some Arab thinkers, writers, and commentators have published in order to explain it and contribute to its overcoming. I must note that I have already expressed some of the thoughts and views included in this study on previous occasions, the most important of them a lecture that I gave at the podium of the Lebanese Club in February 1968 and some essays published in the magazine *Dirasah 'Arabiyya* (Arab Studies) published by Dar al-Tali'ah [Vanguard Press] in Beirut (the issues of August and September 1967 and July 1968).

Sadik Jalal al-Azm
Beirut, August 1968

I

In the first days of the year 1904, a small Asian country that had only recently entered the stage of scientific development, industrial expansion, and modern military organization was able to deal a decisive military blow not only against the largest state in Europe in terms of land-mass, but also a state that was considered at that time one of the strongest naval powers in the world, Russia. Japan gained victory quickly and surprisingly, by the standards of that time, despite the established disparity between the two countries and the known superiority of Russia in all aspects including land area, population, and latent power. Japan achieved its crushing victory with a surprise attack on the Russian fleet in the Pacific Ocean, destroying its ability to wage war and stripping it of its power, which gave Japan total and absolute naval supremacy from the beginning. Remember that in this historical period, naval power had the importance and consequence for states hostile to one another that air power has for our generation today, and that supremacy on the sea meant something very similar to what air supremacy means today in our present wars, especially wars that take place in the desert.

After Japan had annihilated the Russian fleet with its first strike, it was no longer in doubt that the young country would win quickly over old Russia despite its magnitude, because of Japan's progress and Russia's backwardness. Moreover, those who followed the course of the war observed how Imperial Russia overestimated its strength and ability to mobilize in response to that first strike with an even harder strike that would gain for it greater military and political results than it actually achieved. Whoever reviews and examines the facts of history also finds a number of striking similarities between the situation of the Russians and the Japanese in January 1904 and the situation of the Arabs and Israel on the morning of the 5th of June 1967.

If history does not repeat itself in every detail and at every point, this does not mean that historical events do not fall within similar repetitive patterns worth studying and examining closely. Otherwise there is nothing to learn from past experience, no profit gained from the study of the past, and no meanings from history that inform the present.

Let us review some of these similarities: The Tsar, his advisors, and those responsible for guiding the policies of the country were unable to imagine this small country daring to risk a military confrontation with the largest power in Europe. Military intelligence experts declared at that time that if Japan was so mad as to attack Russia, then Russia would respond immediately and confront all Japan's actions without great difficulty.[1] Similar declarations from before the 5th of June continue to ring in our ears, reverberate in our minds, and bring a shudder to our hearts. Russian military intelligence experts made preparations so that Russia would meet the first strike in its central defensive positions and then undertake the strengthening of its forces and launch a sweeping attack that "will push the impudent Asiatics into the sea," to quote their words literally.[2] This self-confidence led to declarations and headlines in the Russian newspapers well represented by the following: "Russia will route the Japanese and bury them under their caps."[3] Expressing the temperament that prevailed in official Russian circles and the governmental bodies, one of the senior Russian officers wrote that "Japan is not a country of the type that can give warnings to Russia. Russia, on the other hand, is obliged not to accept warnings from a country such as Japan."[4] That disdain of the powers of the enemy and this hollow self-confidence resembles nothing so much as what the well-known Arab commentator Mohammed Hassanein Heikal wrote in *Al-Ahram* on June 2, 1967:

> Whatever happens, and without trying to anticipate events, Israel is drawing near almost certain defeat … whether from the inside or the outside.

---

1   Sidney Harcave, *First Blood: The Russian Revolution of 1905* (New York: Macmillan, 1946), 37.
2   Ibid.
3   Ibid.
4   J. A. White, *The Diplomacy of the Russo-Japanese War* (Princeton: Princeton University Press, 1964), 142–3.

It also resembles the following: (a) what a correspondent for the *Al-Jumhuriyya* newspaper wrote on the 21ˢᵗ of May 1967 under the title, "We Can Crush Israel in a Matter of Hours Without Using All of Our Weapons in the Battle;" (b) the assurance that one of the senior officers in the Syrian Arab army expressed in saying that the destruction of Israel will take no more than four days at the maximum; (c) what *Al-Ahram* published in a column estimating the prowess of the Arab and Israeli armies on May 27ᵗʰ, 1967, where it made great efforts to run down the value of Israeli weapons and praise the value of Arab weapons, calling Israeli military prowess a fable propagated by the West and claiming that the enemy army was lacking in unity because it was composed of incongruent bands from every region of the world.

Another similarity between the two wars is that the first masterful strike that destroyed the Russian naval fleet decided the rest of the course of the war, and with startling speed. The same can be said of the first masterful strike that destroyed the Egyptian air force in the most recent war between Israel and the Arabs; however, the second strike decided the fate of the Arab war with Israel with such an unprecedented speed that a BBC correspondent was able to announce the following on the evening of the 5ᵗʰ of June on the "Ten o'Clock News Broadcast":

> After less than fifteen hours after the outbreak of the battle, Israel won the war. Egypt can no longer continue fighting...it is the swiftest victory the modern world has known.[1]

Japan, despite how small it was compared to Russia, had been able to absorb the achievements of modern civilization such as industry, technology, organized scientific research, and technical training, and was able to assimilate them so quickly that it was able to challenge a large state and triumph over it. For Russia, despite its reforms, and attempts at renewal, industrialization, and the assimilation of modern science, remained, in essence, an underdeveloped country, secure in its past and heritage until the war exposed its real position in this domain in comparison to what

---

1   R. S. Churchill, *The Six Day War* (London: W. Heinemann: 1967), 157.

another smaller, aggressive country achieved. It is not necessary that I explain that the comparison between Russian and Japan in 1904 applies in most features and details to any comparison we draw between Israel and the Arab nation in 1968.

After suffering defeat, Russia turned inward, probing itself, re-examining everything, and criticizing itself through the words of its cultural elites, thinkers, artists, political parties, and the enlightened leading factions of the toiling classes. The famous 1905 Revolution was the first of the important direct consequences of the military defeat and the first fruit of the activity of self-examination and self-criticism. Although the 1905 Revolution failed, the strikes and disturbances that followed paved the way for the comprehensive October Revolution, which directed its rage against the inherited traditional models in production, thought, organization, and government, these models that the war put to the test and exposed as obsolescent and inadequate to the demands of modern and contemporary civilization. In other words, Russia was able to transform military defeat from ordeal to constructive experience and from catastrophe to a cultural lesson. It would not have been able to achieve all of this had it not accepted responsibility for the defeat, not attempting to blame anyone but itself, its situation, its organization, and its current status, especially in comparison with the condition and reality of its enemy, the Japanese.

It ought to be clear to the Arabs that their recent defeat resembles the Russian defeat in all aspects, and that it cannot be summed up as merely a transient military loss resulting from political alliances and diplomatic vicissitudes that were not to their advantage, but rather largely to the advantage of their enemy. As in the Russian case, the Arab defeat was tied directly to the prevalent economic, cultural, scientific, and civilizational conditions in the Arab nation, i.e., it was a reflection and expression of those conditions.

I must indicate here a major difference between Russia after the defeat of 1904 and the Arabs after the defeat of 1967. No one who has followed the state of the Arabs before and after the recent war has failed to note our vehement tendency to expend the greatest effort in order to shirk our responsibility and shift it instead onto factors outside our control, allowing us to excuse ourselves for the embarrassing situation we fell into, and for our failure to live up to our obligations in regards to the paramount Arab cause (Palestine) and in regards to modern civilization in general. Although every one of us knows deep down that the responsibility for the defeat, in the end, belongs to us, we persistently attempt in what we say, think, write, and declare to save face, protect appearances, defer to emotions, and concern ourselves with proprieties, morale, flattery, and sensitivities, instead of doing the necessary work of calling things by their names and fixing responsibilities where they belong, saying to the ones who failed "you failed" and to those who are incompetent "you are incompetent."

This tendency to the evasion of self-responsibility has emerged in our claims that American and British airplanes provided a protective umbrella above Israel and participated actively in the strike on our positions. It emerges also in the blame we have poured on the Soviet Union and countries of the socialist bloc immediately after the war, knowing that no country in history lost the major part of its arsenal in the course of a week and then had most of what it lost restored in the course of two months, except the United Arabic Republic [*Egypt's formal name at the time, trans. note*], and the credit for this replacement goes to the Soviet Union. It emerges, too, in the exaggerations we arrive at in order to blame all of the shortcomings in the political and military conditions of the Arabs on colonialism. Some have gone to the extent of dragging in the gods and the unseen to explain and justify the Arab failure, as occurs in the book published recently under the title *Amidat Al-Nakbah* [*Pillars of the Disaster*], where the author says: "The Arabs renounced their faith in God, and God renounced them."[1] As if the relation between man and his God relies on the basis of shared reciprocal needs and common benefits in the manner of "if you abandon me, I abandon you" or "if you love me, I will love you." The Mufti of the Hashemite Kingdom of Jordan, in the course of explaining the Arab defeat and the meanings and moral to be drawn from it to the newspaper *Al-Dustur* (December 22, 1967), stated about the Jews:

---

1   Salah al-Din al-Munajjid, *'Amidat al-Nakbah* [*Pillars of the Disaster*] (Beirut: 1967), 17.

They lack the prowess, boldness, or courage to accomplish these deeds, and we know them better than most others do. However, God desired to impose this group upon us because of our distance from our religion.

In fact, the deviousness of this mode of thinking has reached the point of compassion for the Ottoman state and its caliphate. The author of *Pillars of the Disaster* has written the following in the course of his analysis of the Arab defeat:

> However, the impartial researcher will find that the only fruit of this Arab nationalist and patriotic call is, in the beginning, the destruction of the Ottoman caliphate, and, in the end, remoteness from religion and faith.
>
> The Arabs never gained independence or freedom after the Ottoman defeat and the breaking up of the Ottoman Empire, but instead acquired mandates and protectorates and colonialism, and the Ottoman Muslims became "colonialists" in the view of the nationalists, who adopted the phrase of the Europeans.[1]

Indeed, our use of the term "nakbah" [disaster] to indicate the June War and its aftermath contains much of the logic of exoneration and the evasion of responsibility and accountability, since whomever is struck by a disaster is not considered responsible for it, or its occurrence, and even if we were to consider him so, in some sense, his responsibility remains minimal in comparison with the terror and enormity of the disaster. This is why we ascribe disasters to fate, destiny, and nature, that is, to factors outside our control and for which we cannot be held accountable.

This deviousness in thinking about the defeat and its causes reaches its farthest point in the drivel we find in a book written by Dr. Kamal Yusif al-Hajj (the chair of the philosophy department in the Lebanese University). Dr. al-Hajj asserts in all seriousness that the correct answer to our question, "Why do the Jews persist on

---

1   Ibid. 19.

coming to Palestine," is "because they want to deny the Messiah."[1] The author creates a folk tale out of the Palestinian question and the essence of the Arab-Israeli conflict, emptying it entirely of all its tangible practical and historical contents and making of it, instead, a supernatural-religious problem in which we have no role and are powerless to confront or resist the course of events. The author draws this picture:

> Today, the struggle taking place under our skies is not, in reality, between the Jews and Arabs (as Zionist diplomacy claims), but primarily between the Jews and Jesus Christ.[2]

In fact, this astonishing folk-tale version of the Palestinian question waves a wand to transform the Arabs to a marginal and secondary factor in the "struggle taking place under our skies" and upon the occupied Arab lands. The Arabs stand at the margins of this struggle since Dr. Al-Hajj has discovered the surprising fact that after World Jewry was unable to

> harm Jesus of Nazareth during his life…It has focused all of its cunning to harm his representative on earth. I mean by this His Holiness, the Pope, as the head of the Church.[3]

All I can say is that not even Zionist claims, in their distortion of the Palestinian question, have reached the point of erasing the Arabs from existence as Zionism's sole chief adversary in the historical struggle for the land of Palestine. World Zionism knows who its enemies are and it did not colonize Palestine by rushing into quixotic battle against hidden, supernatural powers that are unidentifiable in the first place.

We regret to find that a progressive Lebanese thinker like Mr. Hussein Muruwwa has been carried away with this current, in the

---

1 Dr. Kamal Yusif Al-Hajj, *Hawla Falsafat al-Sihyuniyya* [*Concerning the Philosophy of Zionism*] (Beirut: 1967), 8.

2 Ibid. 14.

3 Ibid. 9. See also the book of Eliya Abu al-Rus, *Al-Yehudiyyat al-'Alimiyyah wa Harbuha al-Mustimirrah 'ala al-Mesihiyyah* [*World Judaism and its Relentless War against Christianity*] (Beirut: 1964).

beginning at least, and attempted to remove responsibility for the 5th of June from its real source, that is, the Arabs themselves, and their current historical, economic, and cultural situation compared to Israel today. For after he assails those he calls "those spreading doubt" and disparages them with some of the usual disparagements (a fifth column and the like), he says:

> Why, then, are they so eager to spread doubt about the Arab to that extent, is it because of the military defeat that befell him, a defeat for which only very few individuals are responsible, individuals who share nothing with the Arab as a kind but kinship?[1]

Obviously, this sort of talk is pervaded by obscurity and vagueness, and is no help in identifying those really responsible; it instead helps, in an obscure and vague way, to remove responsibility from the Arab as a kind, according to Hussein Muruwwa's expression.

It would be unfair if we did not here make a correction and mention that there is a clear direction now concerning how Arabs speak and think about the 5th of June and its consequences that tends towards backing away from the more exaggerated and extreme flights from responsibility. However, it comes several months late at the official and semi-official levels, and it attempts to treat Arab responsibility for the distressing events of June with great caution and wariness, approaching its acknowledgement with a reluctance, disinclination, and incompleteness that does not reveal real courage or frankness. The most prominent example of this direction are essays that Heikal wrote for *Al-Ahram* that, even several months after the war, never go beyond scratching the surface and never penetrate to the core of this subject. I will adduce several examples in order to make clear what I mean: Heikal acknowledged the role that technical and training shortcomings played in our loss and writes that "modern war is not about the mobilization of the greater amount of weapons, but rather the capacity for using weapons," and quotes what one of the neutral battlefield observers said:

---

1 *Majallat al-Adab* [*Magazine of Literature*] (Beirut: July/August 1967),: 36.

I felt that I had found on the battleground the ruins of a great armed force. However, the hand that directed this armed force was not aware of all its possibilities.[1]

Heikal says:

We were facing a modern and learned foe, and this term alone makes unnecessary all the details that might follow, as it accurately summarizes the elements of superiority that the enemy had achieved.[2]

He then concludes the following:

We face a modern and learned foe, and there is no other solution available to the Arab side at the line of total confrontation but that it be modern and learned.[3]

Or, as he wrote in another place:

Indeed, some of the members of the military leadership entered a condition of nervousness to the point of restlessness...And nervousness also overtook the armed forces and shook it.[4]

It appears to me that this type of acknowledgment of responsibility for Arab shortcomings in regards to the consequences of the 5th of June is not at all of the level to kindle a fresh surge to overcome and surmount the past, and it certainly fails to match the consciousness of responsibility that Russia commanded after its defeat in 1904, especially since our defeat followed its defeat by more than half a century, and since we had two previous experiences with resisting and confronting the Israeli challenge.

In fact, this sort of Arab acknowledgment of responsibility, in my view, has yet to leave behind levels of generality and comprehensiveness that fail to harm anyone, and has yet to detach itself

---

1 *Al-Ahram,* October 6, 1967.
2 *Al-Ahram,* October 20, 1967.
3 Ibid.
4 *Al-Ahram,* October 6, 1967.

from styles of allusion, ambiguity, and models of reluctant, careful, and wary formulation that fail to penetrate to the heart of the matter, that is, to the facts, details, and particulars. Read with us again Heikal's statement: "and there is no other solution available to the Arab side at the line of total confrontation but that it be modern and learned." Just as one of you will not meet an Arab who does not consider himself of the party of charity, motherhood, and "commanding the good and forbidding the bad," so you will not find an Arab who does not consider himself a friend of science, modernity, and progress. At this level of generality and abstraction we all agree and our assent remains compulsory.

However, this sort of talk does us no good unless we pose particular definite questions about science and modernity and what kind of radical changes in ourselves, our societies, and the fabric of our lives will result from them! Are we prepared to accept these changes and transformations, and to renounce all the things that we prized previously, if it is demonstrated that they exert a clear resistance to science and modernity? For science and modernity mean, for example, secularism and the separation of church and state. Who among our responsible leaders dares openly to state this, instead of wrapping the truth inside fine-sounding generalities about science and modernity?

I will give another brief example: Lebanon imports 400,000 crates of whiskey yearly.[1] However, Lebanon still lacks a compulsory official school system that guarantees a free education to all of its children until the end of the secondary stage. Suppose that it is demanded of Lebanon today, in the name of science and modernity naturally, that it sacrifice the greater part of the cost for its 400,000 crates of whiskey imported yearly to finance a comprehensive compulsory education, will the answer be negative or affirmative? I leave the answer to this question to the conscience of each Lebanese, with the reminder that the occupation is ongoing. I will return to the discussion of the question of modern science and its particulars in another section of this study.

---

1   Lebanon, the High Council for Customs, "Foreign Business Statistics."

II

I will shift to a treatment of a number of definite examples that I believe represent the ways in which we shifted away responsibility from ourselves, our institutions, and our present realities for the events of June and their negative effects on the Arabs.

1) Much has been said in describing the June War with Israel as an aggression, and one that relied on elements of deceit and surprise. Let us take a moment to examine closely these descriptions and whether they, in truth, apply to the situation.

The Arabs have and continue to announce persistently that they are in a state of constant war with Israel because its creation was originally an aggression on Arab lands and against Palestinian sovereignty over the occupied land, and this is no doubt and without reservation true for the Arabs. However, can there be, in truth, something by the name of "aggression" when we consider ourselves to be in a constant state of war with the other side, or when we do not recognize the legitimacy of its existence at all? War is war, and while it is possible that there is a breach of a truce agreement that the two sides hold for emergency reasons or a breach of a ceasefire agreement between the two sides for a specified time, what is not possible within a state of war is aggression. For after the June War exposed the dreadful Arab inadequacy in confronting the responsibilities implied by our considering ourselves to be in a state of continual war with Israel, we attempted to conceal that inadequacy and to evade our responsibilities by saying Israel committed aggression against us, as if we had expected from it good neighborliness and fair dealings. Moreover, the concentrated Israeli air attack that destroyed the Egyptian air force and decided the battle from its beginning cannot be considered treachery unless we measure the struggle between ourselves and the Israeli enemy by the standards of a chivalric encounter, where equality of opportunities and armaments is supposed to obtain and where victory in the contest goes to the more courageous and worthy side.

As for war in the second half of twentieth century, what we call treachery has become one of the important techniques of modern war, known as a "surprise attack" in the lexicon of modern military strategy. The response to this tactic has also become well-known in the lexicon of military strategy, and its principle is that a part of our air power, at the first sign that a war is imminent, is to remain in the air constantly and without interruption so that it is not caught una-wares while perching on the ground or on its way up to skies to do battle. While the following of such counter-tactics does not guar-antee victory for the Arabs, it would mean, at least, that while we would have lost the battle, we would not have collapsed in the face of the enemy attack, and would have forced the enemy to pay a very high price for his victory. It appears to me that Arab military think-ing was imagining the modern air war on the order of battles that took place between the German and British aviators in the Second World War, that is, an air battle between formations of planes. In contrast to this Arab military conception, Israel achieved a very modern understanding of air war, surpassing entirely the stage to which the Arabs clung. Dr. Jamal Hamdan summarized this situa-tion by stating: "It was an encounter between the strategies, styles, and arsenals of the Second World War and after on one side, and the strategies, styles, and arsenals of the Third World War on the side of America and Israel.[1]

In other words, emphasizing the element of treachery and surprise will never be able to provide the excuse we seek to exonerate our failure, for the Arab leaders were relentlessly announcing that their efforts were directed at the greater goal, the battle for liberation, and we cannot be surprised by a battle that we wanted and continue to want, prepared ourselves for, and knew was coming without a doubt, whether the enemy wanted it or not. The same can be said for the claims that some Arabs made, that the battle was not equal and fair, in order to evade responsibility and avoid acknowledging our weakness and inadequacy. To repeat, we were not entering a chivalric competition with Israel that imposed on the rival parties respect for equality of opportunities, weapons, and equipment, required a face-to-face encounter, and ruled out surprise and sudden attacks, with victory going to the gallant and just! We instead entered a battle that we advertised as a battle of

---

1   *Al-Katib* [*The Writer*] magazine (Cairo: August 1967).

existence or inexistence, or better, a battle of annihilation, that is, a battle of destiny, and when one is defending his existence or destiny, there is no room for the thoughts of "equality" or "justice," for while it is napalm this time, the next time it may be nuclear bombs.

In reality, the claim that the Israeli attack was treachery not only betrays a farcical attempt to evade responsibility and raise morale but also suggests that the Arabs entered the war with a chivalric understanding of war still holding sway over their minds and reactions. There is nothing more indicative of this than the expressions, thoughts, judgments, and values that we heard in our radio broadcasts and repeated in our newspapers, and in our sayings about the clinking of swords, attack and retreat, and strings of horses, and the personalistic tribal conceptions of the meaning of courage, the defiance of death, honor, zeal, treachery, baseness, and face-to-face confrontation in battle. These are the factors and values that persist in stimulating the emotions of the Arab and inflaming his imagination, despite the fact that he is fighting a battle without direct confrontation, codes of chivalry, and duels. The mainstay of the battle, instead, is the pouncing of airplanes with terrifying speed and extraordinary expertise onto other planes crouching on the ground, and giant armored vehicles ramming against one another and firing on one another according to plans made in military operation rooms. In this kind of war, courage, boldness, and zeal in their traditional meanings play only a small and limited role, and in a war that is decided by napalm bombs and guided rockets whose destructive power cannot be evaded no matter how brave or gallant the individual, chivalric thoughts about gallantry, virility, deception, and baseness cannot play an important role.

We should have made sufficient preparations during the past twenty years for a war in which victory depends on the capacity of the Arab soldier crouched behind an armored device to use its energy and power to the fullest extent possible and on his ability to make quick skilled responses to battle challenges in order to be able to strike the enemy before destruction overtakes him first. However, instead of this, we found ourselves in a war in which Iraqi military units, for example, traveled in broad daylight without air cover or ground protection to the battleground on exposed desert roads, and thus were struck by grave losses. All this in a war on the occasion of which we held numerous celebrations for the military units mobilized for battle where resounding speeches were made, and in so doing our radio stations offered a great service to the enemy intelligence service, sparing it from the required effort of learning the name of the unit, the formation it will answer to in battle, and strength on the battlefield, just as our radio stations even provided Israel the dates of troop movements so that its warplanes bombed them before they reached the battlefield.

We found ourselves in a war in which 'Abd al-Rahman 'Arif [*President of Iraq at the time, trans. note*] told his troops marching to the front to be harsh with the enemy but not to kill a woman or child. Perhaps the rightly-guided caliphs could give this sort of advice to their troops and fighters, but how can our leaders offer the same advice in almost the same words to our troops after the passing of fourteen centuries, while knowing that a large part of the enemy army is composed of women? How can responsible leaders ask the soldier to destroy enemy cities with his planes and bombard villages with his artillery without harming women and children? Naturally, we do not want our solders to commit atrocities or to leave behind massacres; however, this sort of talk from the lips of our leaders gives a strong indication of the nature of the mentality with which we entered the battle and teaches us a hard lesson about it. Moreover, we found ourselves in a war in which the Arab masses were as unprepared as possible for the battle, both psychologically and non-psychologically, since our information agencies planted the thought in all of our heads that a war for the liberation of Palestine was nothing but an "errand" or simple "excursion" to Tel Aviv, with the Arabs afterwards only having to bury the enemy in the sea...and this is the whole matter and this is what the war entails.

In truth, it appears that the mentality that held that the battle for liberation was only an "errand" was not limited to Arab broadcasting circles, but pervaded the highest levels of the Arab leadership. The Jordanian prime minister, who accompanied King Hussein on May 30, 1967 to Cairo to sign the notorious agreement of Arab self-defense, recollected that when the Egyptian president began to discuss with the Egyptian and Jordanian military the capacity of the enemy and the intensity of its preparation, "I imagined, from what Field Marshall 'Amer [*commander of the Egyptian army, trans. note*] said, that the Egyptian armies, supported by the Jordanian troops, would achieve their military aims – were a clash to occur – inside Israel in a matter of days, and that the battle would not amount to more than an easy excursion for these giant imposing forces, and then everything will be over."[1]

Moreover, the tribal, clan, and family ties and values mentioned above that continue to dominate the mentality of the Arabs and determine the patterns of his behavior had dangerous negative effects during as well as after the war on the psychology of the ordinary Arab, on his flight from the occupied territories, and on his incoherent reactions in the face of the Israeli attack. Because of the lack of social institutions, political organizations, and political parties working effectively among the masses, the Arab citizen falls, at the time of sudden danger, under the spontaneous sway of the tribal, behaving in accordance with its norms, and thus feels that his ties to his family or group are stronger than his ties to the "land," and his connection to his tribe, daughters, and relatives is more significant and important than his connection to the threatened "soil of the fatherland."

The study published by the Institute for Palestine Studies about the refugees and the causes of their flight brings full clarity to this aspect of the topic. It is worth mentioning that this study is considered the first scientific empirical inquiry undertaken with Palestinian refugees, and it employed the methodologies of "field studies" and "social surveys," which are well known in the field of social studies. This empirical investigation contains the following facts concerning the effect of tribal values on the behavior of the Arabs in confronting a surprise war and the dangers that threaten their homeland:

> Indeed, family ties are stronger and firmer (than the ties to the land or nation), and these ties have an important impact in the choice to flee rather than stay as we mentioned earlier. In

---

1   Sa`d Jum`ah, *Al-Mu'amarah wa Ma'rakat al-Masir* [*The Conspiracy and the Battle of Destiny*] (Beirut: 1967), 172.

fact, a great number of refugees left in fear for their daughters, women, infants, and young men, rather than in fear for themselves. The truth is that the Arab concept of "sexual honor" played an important role in the process of flight. A refugee whom we spoke with in Zizia refugee camp expressed this role in the following form: "we fled with our sexual honor." In interview after interview, refugee families mentioned that this was among the chief causes for fleeing.[1]

Naturally, no one has brought up these facts in order to blame the defenseless Arab citizen who faces the attacking army while he is under a terrifying shock without any preparation at all (psychological, intellectual, or mental) for dealing with the occupation and its consequences. We admit to a distressing fact only, namely, that the level of social and national maturity among the Arab people, even in the more advanced Arab countries, has yet to transcend the stage of family and tribal allegiance and traditional values, and force the recognition that wars often lead to occupation, violation of sexual honor, and the presence of an occupying army inside the country. However, none of these compel "the flight of the citizens with their sexual honor," and their giving the enemy what it desires, a land empty of inhabitants. The study also demonstrated that the source of this weakness is the lack of social institutions, organizations, and political parties that should take the place of tribal ties in modern national states. As the study states:

> There is also another indirect cause that we believe has great importance, and that is the lack of social ties to institutions, organizations, and political parties. The sole effective tie in Arab society is to the family. In fact, these refugees, for the most part, do not belong to any unofficial institutions, whether religious, political, or social that, when disasters take place, could provide refuge and help them cope. Refugees lacked anyone they can flee to for advice, information, and

---

1 Dr. Halim Barakat and Dr. Peter Dodd, *Al-Nazihuna, Iqtila' wa Nafi* [*The Refugees, Uprooting and Exile*] (Beirut: Institute for Palestine Studies, 1968) 45, 46.

instruction. Social relationships dissolved easily, as if local societies like the village were without centers, or villages and cities were turtles that suddenly lost their shells, leaving flight the only recourse. (page 45)

In other words, responsibility in Arab society still stops at the border of the family and has yet to include the nation as a whole or the homeland in all of its parts. Even within the margins of the family and its narrow values we find a hierarchy of priorities: offspring first, brothers second, offspring of brothers third, offspring of sisters fourth... and the Arab citizen considers himself relatively safe and at peace as long as he, his offspring, his brothers, and the offspring of his brothers and sisters are fed, clothed, and enjoying a reasonable share of their requirements in this life. We know how the Arab citizen living in the cities behaved the eve of the June War when he anticipated the possibility of shortages of some merchandise and foodstuffs offered in the market. Each one of us rushes before all others, and at the expense of every other citizen, to the market, in order to buy and hoard the greatest amount possible of merchandise and foods so that he can afterwards relax considering that he has managed to ensure the needs of his close family even at the expense of the nourishment of others and their deprivation. In truth, this citizen brags among his relatives about his shrewdness and slyness in managing here a sack of flour and there so many kilograms of bread in such grave hours. As long as the family does well, all is well. As for the negative consequences of this type of behavior on the general state of nutrition in the country and on non-relatives whom we leave behind in our shrewdness in hoarding merchandise in our homes, this sort of consideration does not enter our narrow tribal horizons and does not speak to us in the hours of danger and need.[1]

There is no need to append further examples since each of us is capable of drawing them from his own observation of himself and his surroundings.

2) It is difficult for us to find a shortcoming, weakness, or error in

---

1 See the article of Zaki Najib Mahmud, "Muwatin al-Dawlat al-'Asriyyah" ["Citizen of the Modern State"], *Al-Fikr al-Mu'asir* [*Contemporary Thought*] (Cairo: July 1968).

Arab organization, preparation, and planning revealed by the June War that some Arabs have not ascribed to colonialism and international imperialism, often to shift their own responsibility for the defeat in whole and in part to colonialism. However, let us ask ourselves: Did not the Arabs enter the battle of the 5th of June after having prepared for it, and were they not completely aware that Israel had strong and organic ties to colonialism? Truth be told, we knew thoroughly the sort of aid going to Israel, and that Israel, after the Gulf of Aqaba was closed, would take the initiative by administering a harsh military strike, in order to decide the remainder of the battle in its favor. Dayan left no room for doubt about this fact in his news conferences and his various talks just before the battle. Nasser, too, made clear that he was certain that the date of the first Israeli strike would be around the 5th of June. Similarly, the United States left no room for doubt in its intentions towards the Arabs and the extent of its willingness to back Israel, protecting it and its borders. All this was clear to the Arabs and their leadership, and despite all of this, we judged that rushing into battle and gaining victory was within our power. We were wrong, and today it does us no good to blame the other with this vehemence.

Colonialism after the 5th of June is the same colonialism that we experienced and were familiar with before the 5th of June: colonialism cannot be blamed for behaving according to expectations. Wolves are not blamed for behaving like wolves, but rather the objects of blame are those who were supposed to protect the land from wolf attacks but time after time proved that they still lacked the level of effectiveness that would enable them to protect it, despite their boasts and brags.

Another consequence of this logic of exoneration that shifts the blame to colonialism after the 5th of June is a dangerous self-delusion that distinguishes between the power of Israel in itself and the power it draws from others, the inference being that the Arabs will inevitably triumph over Israel when they face its power alone. This distinction between the two types of Israeli power appears in a passage in a lecture given by Chief of Staff Hasan Mustafa in the Arab Cultural Club under the title "Military Lessons from the Setback." He says:

> I have not the slightest doubt that we will triumph over Israel one day, and I am of the highest certainty that our victory over it is historically and logically inevitable. For it is neither reasonable nor natural that a small country like Israel triumphs over all of the Arab nations in the end and that the Arab world as a whole submits forever to its rule and power. The reasonable and rational state of affairs is that the Arabs triumph over Israel since all the factors of natural superiority are on their side.[1]

Perhaps this way of talking seems reasonable, and perhaps the distinction between Israel's own power and the power of others seems valid at the level of theory. However, it loses all its validity when put to the test, since, from the decisive operative standpoint, Israeli power in any battle it enters with the Arabs is all of the power that it is able to deploy in the course of the struggle for victory, no matter what its source. In other words, there is no difference whether it springs from the strip of occupied Palestinian land, the ship "Liberty" on the high seas, or the superiority of the Israeli individual in regards to training, technique, and technology. All Arab resistance to Israel that does not assess its power on that basis remains flawed and farcical since it does not give the full strength of the enemy its due. This includes something of self-deception and self-consolation about the possibility of confronting Israel one day "in itself" or "on its own." We delude ourselves if we expect changes in the world around us to make it possible to isolate Israel "in itself." The best course for us, instead, is to look to change ourselves, our situation, and our society so that we are prepared to confront Israel in all its power, strength, and vitality. The possibilities and powers of the Arab world are certainly much greater than the possibilities and power of the strip of land on which Israel sits; however, reckoning the balance of power in this way is the extreme of foolishness and naiveté, and does no good except to comfort and calm ourselves.

As for what the chief of staff said – "I am of the highest certainty that our victory over Israel is historically and logically inevitable," and "For it is neither reasonable nor natural that a small country like Israel triumphs over all of the Arab nations in the end" – they

---

1   *Al-Thaqafat al-ʿArabiyyah* [*Arabic Culture*] magazine (Beirut: December 1968), 354.

are calming words. However, the recourse to historical and logical inevitability in this matter includes dangers, most importantly, the evasion of bearing responsibility for what happened and the responsibility to define broad plans for what will happen in the light of what actually happened. This talk of inevitability also contains another danger, the inference that the state of the Arabs is essentially sound, since it was not responsible for what happened on the 5th of June (colonialism, for example, is the guilty party). Thus persisting in the same course will not harm the Arabs since the nature of things and historical events in their inevitable path will lead them in the end to victory over Israel.

Perhaps it does not appear reasonable that a small country like Israel triumphs over the Arabs in the end. However, history is not always obligated to what might appear reasonable and natural to people in a particular period. It is not reasonable that Japan triumphed over Russia, but it did; it is not reasonable that the Egyptian air force be crippled by one strike, but this is what happened; and it is not reasonable that a very small country like Great Britain ruled over an empire on which the sun never set, with its extensive surface area, latent powers, and tremendous number of inhabitants, but Britain managed this for three centuries. So while it is neither reasonable nor natural that the Arabs have been defeated by Israel three consecutive times in less than a quarter century, this is what has happened. It appears, then, that our metrics for what is reasonable and natural are subjective and delusional, not objective and scientific. What is important is that the danger alluded to by the chief of staff concerning the triumph of a small state like Israel over the sum of Arab states continues to be a standing danger and that we should not allow ourselves to minimize it by explaining it away with an appeal to reasonability, logic, or historical inevitability. For none of these, in the end, exclude the possibility of the worst and most distasteful course of events becoming an abiding historical truth.

The issue, then, is not resolved by casting blame on the colonialism that created and established Israel, but in transforming the Arab people and society into effective powers capable of taking responsibility for confronting colonialism as embodied in Israel.

The issue is the extent of our capacity to transform the truths we knew about colonialism before the 5th of June into a part of an Arab strategy that works at the level of practical implementation and tangible reality. There is nothing more indicative of our incapacity to do that than the following instance: when the political leadership in Cairo took its final decision concerning the necessity of bearing the brunt and absorbing the first Israeli military strike on the basis of its full knowledge of the intentions of the colonialists towards the Arabs and of the intentions of Israel to launch a surprise attack, the executive apparatus, as emerged afterwards, was entirely incapable of carrying out this decision. It was unable to translate it into reality, that is, into practical measures ensuring the mitigation of that first strike to the greatest extent possible and into practical steps to contain its after-effects and limit them to the narrowest scope, enabling the Arab forces afterwards to launch a corresponding counter-attack that would ensure a more favorable military result, if not total victory.

Whether we turn the blame on colonialism or not, the basic issue remains the effectiveness of the Arab people and society in confronting present challenges and dangers. There is no doubt that Arab underdevelopment in production, technology, science, planning, and leadership is the latent source, to a great extent, of the lack of this sort of practical effectiveness among the Arabs today. The young revolutionary Régis Debray identifies the future course of action in the following words:

> Our task, in sum, is the struggle for effectiveness. The search for effectiveness draws together everyone who has a speck of conscience, and all means possible in a field where, fortunately, pure theory does not have the primary place...After all of these years of empty phrases, lying promises, and unrealized programs, there is an urgent need for effectiveness: it almost strikes the door with vehemence. However, if this need is not coupled with intelligence, it will not bear fruit.[1]

3) One of the more significant of the prevalent styles in rationalizing the defeat and shifting responsibility to the other is the widespread

---

1   Régis Debray, *Thawrah fi'l-Thawrah* [*Revolution in the Revolution*] (Beirut: Dar Al-Adab, 1968), 19.

view that if Cairo had taken the initiative in the beginning and struck the Israeli air force in the way that Israel struck the Egyptian air force, then the situation would be reversed and the Arabs would have won. That is, the difference between victory and defeat in this war depended on nothing but a political decision or simple mistake in assessment. If we undertook, then, on the morning of the 4th of June what Israel undertook on the 5th, our army would now be in Tel Aviv. This logic of rationalization means, first, that the condition of the Arabs is sound and that the defeat was merely the result of overpowering but trivial political circumstances, that we either neglected or failed to take into consideration. However, the question arises: May we assume, given what we now know about the war, that the Arab air force had reached the level of effectiveness that would allow it to execute the plan of attack with the accuracy, mastery, speed, and proficiency that characterizes the Israeli air force in its attack on the air bases of the United Arab Republic? In the lecture mentioned earlier, Chief of Staff Hasan Mustafa states with full clarity the following:

> That the Arab military forces undertook the attack before the enemy does not entail by itself our success in the attack or certain victory over the enemy. For in order for our attack to succeed we would have to have mastered every aspect of this kind of military assault.[1]

After the lecturer analyzed in detail the necessary factors for success in the plan of attack and explained how the Arab forces had not, in fact, reached the necessary level of effectiveness to succeed in an assault operation of this sort, he says literally: "Unless all or most of these factors are present, we might fail and our attack turn into a massacre."[2]

---

1 *Al-Thaqafat al-'Arabiyyah* [*Arabic Culture*] magazine (Beirut: December 1968), 362.
2 Ibid. 362. Heikal acknowledged this fact a year after the defeat when he mentioned that an Arab victory was not possible even if the United Arab Republic had initiated the attack on Israel. He says, "The surprise of the morning of the 5th of June destroyed the air force on the ground in hours. Most probably and on the basis of the objective circumstances alone, even without the surprise, the air force would have been destroyed in the air during the next days, because of the conditions under which it entered the battle." *Al-Ahram* (June 28, 1968). Just as he also says, "A

These styles of rationalizing Arab failure and evading responsibility and accountability have cost us dearly in the past and present, and I mean in particular that the purges that some Arab armies witnessed after the 5th of June, especially in the army of the United Arab Republic, should have been carried out after the Suez War in 1956. However, the political victory we achieved in the Suez War dazzled us and convinced us that the Israeli assault on the Sinai at that time was not the result of any weakness in our military or failing in our present situation. Chief of Staff Hasan Mustafa makes this clear in his lecture when he says:

> It appears that the political victory that Egypt achieved as a consequence of the Suez War against the French-British-Israeli aggression caused its military leaders to forget their tactical errors in that war, and thus they neglected to remedy these defects and failed to deal with many of the weakness of leadership and training. Similarly, they seem to have belittled the military capacity of Israel and its military successes in the Sinai Desert in 1956, attributing all of them to the participation of Great Britain and France alongside it in the war.[1]

4) One of the indications of the self-delusory character of the rationalizations and excuses that we have observed after the 5th of June in our magazines and newspapers, particularly in some Beirut newspapers, is the constant clamor that Israel defiled sexual honor, violated the sanctity of the mosques, and stole the precious crown from the head of the statue of the Virgin Mary, and that it has imprisoned, exiled, suppressed, and tortured. These claims

---

fundamental fact appears clearly now after a year...that any Arab victory would have been difficult during those days of 1967." *Al-Anwar* (June 21, 1968). One ought not let this acknowledgment of the impossibility of an Arab victory casually pass by the attention of the Arab citizen, because behind it hides – despite how Heikal only mentions and acknowledges it briefly and in passing – a frightening truth about the relations and connections between the Arab masses and their leadership, political organizations, and communications services in the period following the French-British-Israeli aggression in the Suez Canal. That is, the misled Arab popular masses were in one camp, and the regimes, organizations and institutions that should have represented them were isolated in another camp. In these awful circumstances, the defeat should come as no surprise.

1   Ibid. 375.

comprise an attempt to cover up the embarrassing situation of the Arabs by slandering and disparaging the enemy, and illustrating its pettiness, as if this clamor and cursing will have any effect on it, or change the fact of its power and the reality of its strength. Not to mention that it reduces the noble nationalist battle facing the Arabs to the level of pettiness, sophistry, and scorn, and throws over us a negative shadow, since when we disparage the enemy and diminish his status, we make our defeat appear worse and more disgraceful than it actually was. For a despicable and low enemy (instead of a worthy one) robs us of every sound rationalization for being defeated.

In any case, how does it profit us that we exaggerate Israeli deeds, magnify its actions, or inflate them to such an extent over our own internal fronts? Did we expect better or finer behavior from the Israeli army of occupation? Or were we ready for celebrations, rejoicing, and praise when victory appeared imminent and unable to bear the expected consequences of war when we lose? Let us remember that the enemy army is an army of occupation and its primary task is to strike down any Arab resistance in the harshest and most ruthless manner, just as the task of Arab resistance and its primary obligation is a relentless effort to drive it from the occupied lands and give it a bitter taste of its fierceness, harshness, and cruelty. We have no right to behave as if we expected something other from an occupation army than torture, harshness, suppression, and carnage. Are we so naïve that we expect from "the gangsters' statelet," as we used to call it, something other than gang behavior, or that we expect from it compliance with the law of human rights?

If in our hours of elation and high aspirations, Israel is the aggressor state, then why do we behave as if it is something else in our hours of sadness and grief? To preserve our composure as individuals and our attitude as a group, we ought not to be struck by surprise when an occupying army behaves like occupying armies do. Let us remember that the harshness of Israeli oppression is the best and most accurate measure and indication of the fierceness of the Arab resistance – the proportion between them is a package.

This clamor has reached its crescendo in our attitudes towards the occupation of the city of Jerusalem. Our press has surrounded the old city of Jerusalem with a special halo and given it a central place that distinguishes it, for some reason, from the rest of usurped, occupied, and lost land. Moreover, it has written much about its lost importance to tourism, especially in relation to Lebanon. It appears to me that this thinking contains a dangerous delusion because it strives to favor one part of the occupied land over the other parts, which indirectly supports the calls for the internationalization of Jerusalem, and gives the general impression that one part of Palestine is dearer to us than the other parts, or that for the sake of one part we might renounce our claims to other parts, or that we insist on the liberation of an old Arab city before the other parts of the occupied territory. Nothing distinguishes old Jerusalem from any other inch of occupied Arab land in absolute terms. In this respect, nothing distinguishes it from grains of sand in the Sinai, or Nablus, or Quneitra, or Haifa, or Jaffa. Yes, we might expect some propaganda gains abroad because of the religious status of Jerusalem. However, we must be completely clear with ourselves about the truth of this situation and recognize that just as the Algerian people did not struggle and sacrifice just in order to enjoy the ceremonies of raising the flag and the singing of national anthems, so our struggle against the occupation of Palestine is not summarized by the return of mosques and churches that attract tourists.

It is one thing to say propaganda gains abroad are very important for our case. However, it is another thing to accept the logic of rationalization and the evasion of responsibility, asserting that we lost because our propaganda did not draw international public opinion to our side. The peoples and governments of the states advanced in industry and culture, whether in the socialist or capitalist bloc, find a kind of sympathy, understanding, and kinship between themselves and a state such as Israel that has made great progress in science, industry, and technology. That is, these states and peoples see in Israel and its accomplishments a microcosm of themselves, an extension of their culture and of everything that they consider technical, scientific, and modern accomplishments. Zionist propaganda has reinforced this factor, by presenting Israel as an advanced, lively, dynamic society that shares in the enriching of the modern scientific, cultural, and literary heritage, like the advanced societies in both Western and Eastern Europe. Even the developing countries and their peoples have begun to look to Israel as a pioneering experiment in this area, from which they can learn and profit. Intensifying Arab propaganda abroad will not change anything in this picture. It appears to me that the emergence of one first-class Arab mind in the realm of the natural sciences, or the flourishing of one Arab scientific institution at the level of the Israeli Weizman Institute, or Arab participation in enriching the contemporary scientific and literary inheritance in a way that is continuous, increasing, and cumulative, or the invention of a modern Arab weapon that is effective because it suits the conditions of our struggle, or the emergence of one Arab military mind at the level of General Giáp [*commander in chief of the People's Army of Vietnam, trans. note*] would save us an enormous fund of money that is being spent in the name of a propaganda that does not rest on real foundations or achievements. The achievements I enumerated, by way of examples, will do wonders to change the image that peoples and states have of our conditions and abilities. There can be no disagreement that the Arabs have fallen very short in this vital area, if we compare them to other underdeveloped countries that were able to absorb, in a short time, the achievements of modern culture in its science, technology, and organization, and from there to shift from taking advantage of the fruits of science, importing its practical applications, and using them in a shallow manner, to making creative scientific contributions and enjoying a comprehensive renaissance in all areas. This is the truth of our situation, in spite of the fact that a relatively long time has passed since the contact of the Arabs with modern cultural achievements, some going back to Napoleon's Egyptian campaign, and although the Arab states have never ceased to send missions to the European countries in order to profit from elements of modern culture and introduce them into Arab society.

I feel compelled to mention in this regard a matter I observed when I visited Damascus in the past month of Ramadan because it explains to me, as simple as it is, the aftermath of the 5th of June to a much higher degree than everything that has been written or said until today in commenting on, explaining, or rationalizing the defeat. I observed there a socialist country in which the state is considered the largest employer of the people and in which it is assumed that the state is the axis of production, work, and construction, and the chief engine of continual progress. However, despite all of this, the period of official work for all state employees and officials did not exceed four hours a day, that is, from ten in the morning until two in the afternoon, out of respect for the month of Ramadan and the duty of fasting. What will happen to the Israeli economy if the government decides to squander half the workday for only a week, not the whole month? Any capitalist country embarking on such a step, even for one week, would topple immediately into a harsh financial crisis. How would things be, then, with a country passing through the stage of socialist transformation, where the state is everything, in all meanings of the word?

Socialist Syria stands in the line of fire, this is one aspect. As for another, it is clear that if Syria works four or six or eight hours in the day, everything will remain the same and no one will notice a difference, and this matches entirely how I felt during the past month of Ramadan. This phenomenon alone holds meanings, significance, and implications concerning the truth of the Arab social situation that suffice to explain the Arab defeat without searching for other causes.

5) There is a very simple and popular explanation among Arab citizens, despite differences in views and status, which ascribes the consecutive Arab defeats at the hands of Israel to International Zionist control over the world as a whole, and over the resources of countries and nations, and even over the course of modern history in its entirety. This type of interpretation emerged with special emphasis after the defeat in numerous Arabic books and articles that presented the idea in styles and forms with differing levels of immaturity and naïveté. As an example, Dr. Kamal Yusif al-Hajj, in his book referred to earlier, confirms that "capitalism is also a matter under the control of World Jewry"[1] and that "revolutionary socialism is also among the Jewish intellectual creations."[2] Similarly, he titles one of the chapters in his book "Socialism is the Stepdaughter of the Zionists."[3]

---

1   *Hawla Falsafat al-Sihyuniyya* [*Concerning the Philosophy of Zionism*], 79.
2   Ibid. 80.
3   Ibid. 77.

There are also other writers who seek refuge in the *Protocols of the Elders of Zion* to prove that the Jews practice total control, through infernal international conspiracies, over the course of modern history (and perhaps ancient history, too). According to this superstitious logic, the Elders of Zion gather together at least once every century where they carry out discussions and studies in order to compose their frightening secret plan to enslave the world. The creators of this "theory" of historical explanation assure us that the course of history proceeds, without the least doubt, according to the plans of the conspiracy. It does not deviate an inch because of the cleverness of the Jewish leaders and their excessive intelligence and unlimited influence, which makes them masters of planning and implementation for a century at a time with an unimaginable efficiency.[1] This imaginary pattern of thinking and planning takes on an almost reasonable and serious character – at best – when it seeks to explain American policy (or the capitalist West in general) by asserting that the Jews rule over the American economy, oversee the society of that country, and direct its policies and positions to their advantage and the advantage of Israel. Thus they insist on the role of the Jewish vote in American political life and in imposing a particular direction to its foreign policy. The following are my critical observations on this widespread model of thinking about the defeat and about the Palestinian question in general.

Of the terrible errors that the Arabs have fallen into as far as their cause is concerned, the first is the extreme underestimation of the capacity of the enemy. The second terrible error that the Arab appraisal of Zionism and its power has fallen into is the exaggeration of its power and influence, to the extent of ascribing it overwhelming mythical powers that make it the mistress of capitalism, socialism, and the course of history at the same time. Naturally, exaggerating the power, strength, and influence of the enemy in this fantastic manner is one of the ways to rationalize our failure and shift responsibility for the defeat on factors outside of our power, especially since these factors belong to forces that we want to believe are of such greatness and magnitude that they render

---

1   Shawqi 'Abd al-Nasir, *Brutukulat Hukama' Sihyun wa Ta'lim al-Talmud* [*Protocols of the Elders of Zion and the Teaching of the Talmud*] (Cairo: Dar al-Ta'awun), 43, 50.

impotent even the courage of the most courageous. Then can the Arabs be blamed for failing to respond in kind to the Zionist challenge after the defeat, since they were facing a power they imagined was the master of life and fate in, at the least, both the capitalist and socialist blocs?

The diffusion of this kind of thinking among the Arabs to explain their defeat by Zionism and its colonialist allies indicates that the Arab mind (or better, the Arab imagination) still leans strongly towards the adopting of the simplest and most naïve explanations for the course of historical events. The simplest way to understand a complicated phenomenon like the foreign policy of a country like the United States is to ascribe it to some individuals or a group of individuals (the Elders of Zion, for example) whom we can hold entirely responsible and on whom we can heap blame, inferring that if they disappeared from existence, then the course of events would alter entirely. In other words, we always search for an explanation for events that returns in the end to a "willpower" behind them or to projected "intentions and goals" of individuals who organize the course of events according to their whims and in complete secrecy. According to this logic, the course of history for the period of a century, for example, tracks exactly the goals, intentions, and will of, for instance, the Elders of Zion, secluded in secret. The Arab mind is not yet familiar with the explanation of events according to modern scientific methods that do not rely on final causes and do not seek the source of events in concealed wills and personalized powers, but rely instead on objective economic considerations, for example, or social forces either in an automatic manner or interacting among themselves in a dialectical way, among others. The Arab imagination still prefers to explain the policies of the United States by referring to an evil murky band of conspirators with control over everything instead of explaining it on the basis of American economic and strategic interests and the defense of enormous American capitalist investments in a region that includes both the Middle East and Southeast Asia in their entireties. It is obvious that this reigning model of interpretation is a product of the influence of mythological or traditionally religious thinking that explains events, in the end, by recourse to divine will and the desires of supernatural beings, and that sees in the course of history a premeditated plan for the path of events and an intentional design for everything that happens.

It is certain that the propagandists of this great exaggeration of World Zionist power and influence in the manner of Dr. al-Hajj strive for particular goals that can be summed up as the exoneration of the capitalist West, in general, and the United States, in particular, from the charge of a crude premeditated hostility towards the Arab cause in Palestine. The logic of these propagandists runs in the direction of saying that the will of the West is incapacitated by the domination that Zionism exercises over it, and so that we should not blame the West for its hostile positions against us because it is really deceived, compelled, and unfree. In other words, the "West" is the natural ally of the Arabs and their interests, and if we explain to it how Zionism exploits it to advance its own interests, then it will regain its senses and revert from this seduction. Hence there is no reason for hostility towards the West since it is originally innocent. Dr. al-Hajj says:

> I believe that the Arab peoples are mistaken in believing the West is primarily responsible for Zionism.[1]

Then he describes this Arab conviction as superficial and a distortion of the truth in order to conclude:

> I do not blame the West because it has been deceived, exactly as we have been deceived all these times: Yes, the West is deceived.[2]

The natural consequence to this startling logic is to place great responsibility on the shoulders of the Arabs to awaken the West from its slumber, as Dr. al-Hajj puts it. After completing the rescue operation, we become (by some miraculous power, naturally) "the possessors of the West instead of the Zionists being its possessors...this awesome Western power falls within our grasp instead

---

1 *Hawla Falsafat al-Sihyuniyya* [*Concerning the Philosophy of Zionism*], 127.
2 Ibid. 128.

of the grasp of the Zionists."[1] Our pity should, then, go to the poor deceived West instead of the poor Palestinian cause that falls into the snares of this appalling right-wing fairy-tale logic. It is clear from this how unadulterated reactionary thinking seeks refuge in scaremongering concerning the irresistible power and influence of World Zionism in order to return the Arabs, in principle, to the fold of the West, economically and politically, this innocent, deceived, unfortunate West!

As for those who explain American policy concerning the Palestinian question on the basis of the Jewish votes and the influence the Jewish minority enjoys in the offices of the government, they are also striving (whether they acknowledge it or not) to exonerate America, as a country with wide colonialist interests, from the accusation of open hostility to the Palestinian cause and the causes of the Arab nation in liberation from foreign economic control and dependence on world capitalism. This group of people does not want to attribute American policy to basic American positions arising from its enormous colonialist interests extending to all continents, but wants to attribute it instead to political factors like the Zionist influence resulting from many factors, among them the votes of the Jewish minority in American elections, in order to mitigate the situation a bit. Of course, according to this logic, if half the American Jews left the country, for example, and, consequently, their influence shrunk in the same proportion, American positions would shift halfway toward the direction of the Arab side in the Palestinian question and otherwise. Why not? Is not America a democratic country in which the electoral vote decides everything? However, these preconceptions partial to non-Jewish America are one thing, and the truth is something else. If the number of Jewish votes shrunk to half, that certainly would not change the core of the American stance towards Israel, the Palestinian cause, and the Arab reactionary regimes in general, because the deepest roots of the American stance are in its very vital interests (from Arab oil to the tin, tungsten, and rubber of Southeast Asia, and then its enormous important investments in countries with cheap manual labor), and these factors are much more important than the desire

---

1 Ibid. 128.

of the candidates to satisfy the demands of the American Jewish minority.

It suffices that we mention here that the Jewish minority in America was never content with Eisenhower's policy towards the French-British-Israeli aggression against Egypt in the year 1956 (this does not mean that the Arab movement for liberation was satisfied with the policies of Eisenhower and Dulles) because it believed "that the Eisenhower government was much less mindful of the friendship with Israel than Truman's was."[1] However, despite this, Eisenhower entered the White House with a crushing popular majority unprecedented in the history of the United States presidency. Just as when Hitler organized his appalling massacres of the Jews in Germany and the regions that it occupied, the votes of the American Jews with all their influence failed to convince the government to open the door to immigration for the groups of Jews fleeing from oppression. Despite the clarity of these truths, we still find thinkers like Walid Khalidi insisting on discussing and explaining American policy and positions by recourse to the consideration of electoral politics alone. Walid Khalidi says the following in explaining the motives of American policy:

> I do not imagine that it is unclear to anyone that the original motivation to which I am referring is the electoral political considerations [of America's political elite]. Consequently, it is possible to understand America's Palestinian policies as, at bottom, a reflection of the immorality of America's political elite, generation after generation.[2]

In our view, this explanation remains superficial and incomplete because it looks to the "considerations of electoral politics" and the "immorality of American political elites" as if they are final and irreducible realities that cannot be attributed back to deeper factors and more entrenched interests in American society, which allow

---

1   Mustafa 'Abd al-'Aziz, *Al-Aqaliyyat al-Yehudiah f'il Wilayat al-Mutihadat al-Amrikiyah* [*The Jewish Minority in the United States of America*] (Beirut: PLO Research Center, 1968), 119.

2   "Filastin 'Am 1968" ["Palestine in the Year 1968"] *Al-Thaqafat al- 'Arabiyyah* [*Arabic Culture*] (Beirut: July/August 1968), 212.

us to explain these political phenomena and explicate the causes shaping them. Do the American elites behave "immorally" because, for some reason, they are disposed by nature to reprehensible moral qualities or because they are defending an enormous network of capital, investments, corporations, bank branches, markets, and raw materials in almost every corner of the world?

As for the tale of the control of the Jews on the American economy, their mastery over the society, and their determination of the policy of the country, it is closer to myth than it is to the truth. The Arabs are fond of this tale in order to explain away everything that displeases them about the strength, resoluteness, and boldness of Israel and to exonerate themselves from their lack of effective resistance to the constant encroachments of Israel on Arab lands. We are fond of this tale, without examining the facts and realities, although it covertly exonerates non-Jewish America from most of the accusations we have turned and still turn towards it, shifting the blame from America to the one small group assumed to enjoy the greatest influence and hegemony there.

In order to determine the truth of this story of Jewish domination over the American economy we need only return to the data presented in the book I cited earlier, *Al-Aqaliyyat al-Yehudiah f'il Wilayat al-Mutihadat al-Amrikiyah (The Jewish Minority in the United States of America)*. After close examination of the facts presented in this work, it is apparent that Jewish interests only dominate some limited regions of the middle sectors of the American economy, and thus fall short of controlling general economic activity in the country. The following are some examples of economic areas that submit to the influence of the Jews, either partly or as a whole: the manufacture of men's and women's apparel almost as a whole; the fur industry; fashion, design, and cosmetics; wholesale and retail trade in some merchandise types; jewelry; the grocery business; spirits, import and export; the film industry and the media in general, including publishing houses.[1] Just as the Jews enjoy a strong influence as stockbrokers (especially in New York) and in professional areas such as law, medicine, dentistry, and university teaching. However, all of these economic sectors falling

---

1 *Al-Aqaliyyat al-Yehudiah f'il Wilayat al-Mutihadat al-Amrikiyah*, 49, 51, 54.

under Jewish control are nothing but drops in the sea in comparison to the basic sectors that form the sensitive nerve of the American economy, where we find the source of real political power. Let us include some examples of the companies that American society thrives with or fades with: Standard Oil and the other oil companies; Dupont; large steel companies from U.S. Steel (the largest) to Bethlehem Steel (the sixth in size); in the area of money transfers and banks, Bank of America, Chase Manhattan Bank, First National City Bank; the famous large airline companies; the main automobile manufacturers; the big advertising companies; agribusiness; and so on until the end of the list.

The truth is that the group that controls this sector of the economy controls, consequently, the American economy and society in general. There is not the slightest doubt that the Jews lack influence in this main sector – they are not allowed to approach it at all, and thus cannot dominate it. The group with hegemony in the American economy is the "White Protestants," as they are called in the United States, or WASPs, the acronym for White Anglo-Saxon Protestants. However you look, you will not find the Jews (or even Catholics) having any real power or influence worth mentioning in these sensitive centers or leadership in any of the institutions or companies that I have cited. In a similar way, the names of the companies themselves carry well-known Protestant Anglo-Saxon family names like Dupont, Ford, and Chrysler, with the Rockefeller family maintaining control of the Chase Manhattan Bank. Anyone seeking additional certainty about this topic need only review the names of the members of the boards of directors and senior executives in these large companies and giant banks in order confirm the extent of the power and influence of the Jewish minority in them. Naturally, we do not claim at all that the Jews in America are not powerful, rich, and carry great influence in the halls of government; however, this is one thing and the charge that they control the American economy is something else. Mustafa 'Abd al-'Aziz states the following on this topic:

> Few Jews are found who own steel mills or even work in them, and likewise few of them work in the petroleum refinery business, mining, automobile manufacturing or repair, or

meat packing, canning, and preservation, among other major industries. There are few Jews who work as either employees or owners in public utilities such as railroads, electricity, gas, and the like. Though the number of them who work in senior executive positions in banks is relatively small, they have a great influence in publishing houses, printing, broadcasting, television, and the film studios.[1]

The author notes himself the scarcity of Jews working in banks, saying:

> It appears that in 45 of these banks, there is not a single Jewish employee at the senior level. In four of them, there is only one Jew at the senior level. In one bank there are four Jews in the higher positions and only 32 Jews out of the 3438 employees found in middle management.[2]

Moreover, the great bane of American social life is its racial discrimination and notorious ethnic chauvinism. The essential source of this deep tendency is the White Protestant group that has true power over the economy. Racial discrimination is not only aimed at blacks, but also American Indians, Jews, Puerto Ricans, Mexicans, the Chinese, the Japanese, and even Catholics from Italy and Ireland. On this basis, we can see clearly the existing relation between White Protestant economic hegemony, on the one hand, and the racial discrimination it practices against other groups who either control little (like the Jews), or those who have no power at all worth mentioning (and for whom it is not desired that they gain control of anything) like blacks, American Indians, and Puerto Ricans.[3] Therefore, we find

---

1 Ibid. 62–3.
2 Ibid. 103.
3 Here we find the true explanation for the aversion of the Jews towards Eisenhower. Eisenhower, in fact, was no more sympathetic to the Arab cause than other presidents of the United States. As evidence, consider the entirely hostile positions of his government (especially Dulles) towards the issues of the day in this period like positive neutralism, non-alignment, Egypt's breaking of the Western armament monopoly, the building of the Aswan Dam, or the policy of Western alliances, the famous "vacuum theory," policies of containment and encirclement, and the nuclear deterrent that his government applied against the Soviet Union and the

that although Jewish students fluctuate between 10 and 12 percent of the total college student population in America, and despite deep Jewish penetration into university teaching, Jews are rarely found working in high administrative positions in universities and colleges such as university president or dean of an important faculty.[1]

We conclude from this discussion the following points:

First: The prevalence of the delusion of total Jewish domination of the American economy and its wide circulation among Arab citizens is a result, at best, of ignorance of American economic conditions and facts, and of our wish to adopt a quick and simple explanation for American behavior towards the Palestinian cause. At worst, it is a deliberate attempt to clear non-Jewish America (in other words, the actual America with its extensive economy, interests, colonialism, etc.) from responsibility for hostile actions against the Arab nation and for its active participation in the driving out of the Palestinian Arab people.

---

socialist bloc in general. The aversion of the Jewish minority, then, did not have its source in his reputed sympathy for the Arab cause in and beyond Palestine. The underlying reason for this aversion was the reputation of his government as being the representative, in all clarity and without any duplicity, of the interests of the big economic sectors in America at the expense of the smaller sectors. The ordinary American expresses this by saying that the Eisenhower administration leaned more than others did towards serving the interests of Big Business and that this was at the expense of relatively small businessmen. Since the large economic sectors are in the hands of the "White Protestants" and largely shielded from Jewish influence, it is, then, no wonder that the Jewish minority in America was not in full agreement with Eisenhower and his government, especially with Dulles, he being from the pure "White Protestants" and their primary representative in the government and state. In truth, the Jews did not support the Republican party because it was known for its very conservative leanings in social and economic areas, springing from its strong ties with elements of Big Business, and because Republican party rule means strengthening the barriers against the Jews and their influence from entering the large economic sectors and their dependencies. In spite of that most of the votes of the Jews went, therefore, to the candidate of the Democratic Party, Eisenhower won, as everyone knows, with a crushing majority, that is, the votes of the Jews did not have any effect on the results, as I mentioned above.

1   *Al-Aqaliyyat al-Yehudiah f'il Wilayat al-Mutihadat al-Amrikiyah* [*The Jewish Minority in the United States of America*], 70. To become familiar with other aspects of the discrimination against the Jews, see page 110.

Second: The Arab conception of the Zionist movement either as an extension and a dependant of America or as ruling and controlling America contains a significant oversimplification of the historical facts, since the history of the Zionist movement shows that it formed alliances with powerful states according to its current interests and present conditions. For that reason, Herzl tried to rely on Kaiser Wilhelm II in the beginning (1898), and when that failed, tried to approach the Ottoman state (1901), failing in his efforts again. In 1902, the Zionist movement began to rely on Great Britain, which was convinced that the Jewish state would be a shield and ally for it and its interests against the Arabs and its rivals at the time like France. All of this we know from the Balfour Declaration. The Arabs said during those years, and afterwards, what is said today about the relation of the Zionist movement to America, that is, that Zionism ruled Great Britain and controlled it and its economy. They also said that it was no more than an extension and a dependant of Great Britain. As for the story of the transition of the Zionist movement during the Second World War to America, it is widely accepted that since the United States became the most powerful state in the world and began to extend its interests to the Middle East, it was only natural that America profit from the Zionist movement as completely as Great Britain did before it. In other words, the American and Zionist wills fell into harmony, in an almost complete agreement about goals and vital interests in the Middle East in this historical period.[1]

Third: The deciding factor in determining America's Palestinian policy is the vital interests of America (in all their kinds) that extend to every corner of the world: the factors that ultimately determine its policy in Latin America and Vietnam also determine the pattern of its policies in the Middle East, where this policy takes on the shape of supporting Israel and the reactionary regimes and trying to fight all of the liberation movements that may have the audacity to eliminate American interests and threaten its security, stability,

---

1 Adhal Hussain, "Al-Tariq al-Muwajahat al-'Adwan wa Tasfiyat al-Kiyan al-'Ansari fi Isra'il" ["The Way to Confront Aggression and the Elimination of the Racist Nature of Israel"] *Al-Tali'ah* [*Vanguard*] magazine (Egypt: July 1967), 106–10.

and expansion of influence. Unfortunately, the defeat of the 5th of June showed the extent of American political success in the Middle East, since it gained immensely from the almost lethal strike that the Arab revolutionary movements suffered, just as it succeeded in reviving the region's traditional regimes and in fortifying Israel with a new strategic dimension, all of this without any disturbance of vital American interests in the Arab world, and while maintaining all its previous petroleum-related, financial, strategic, and cultural prerogatives.

Fourth: Since the support of the new colonialist states to Israel is proportional with the size of the colonialist interests in the Arab world, and since the Arab inability to confront Israel is also pro-portional to the influence of the colonialist states in the economy and politics of a large portion of the Arab states, we may infer that the battle to eliminate the colonialist influence in the Arab world and the building of a modern socialist society are entirely comple-mentary, and that they are inseparable from the Arab struggle to confront Israel and liberate the occupied land.

III

After this examination and analysis of the specific examples of the tendency to shift responsibility away from oneself and to project it on others that appeared so clearly after the defeat of the 5th of June, I want to insist that this tendency is bound with basic factors that belong to the structure of traditional Arab society and are inseparable from characteristics of the social per-sonality that the inherited Arab milieu instilled and developed in each of us. While it is not within my ability to expand on this aspect of the subject, I want to tie the appearance of the Arab logic of exoneration that we worked through with a pattern of particular social behavior that the well-known Arab social scien-tist Dr. Hammed 'Ammar studied and gave the name "the clever personality [al-shaksiat al-fahlawiyyah]."[1] The clever personality is nothing but an abstraction and pattern, and does not exist in living reality except in the shape of characteristics, patterns of behavior, reactions, and sensibilities that describe individuals in a specific social environment and to different degrees, sometimes increasing, sometimes decreasing, from one individual to another according to circumstances and conditions.

One of the properties of the clever personality that Dr. 'Ammar enumerates is the constant search for the shortest and fastest route to realize particular goals and aims while avoiding the toil and the effort usually required in overcoming impediments to reach this goal, and avoiding using the natural means to attain it, because the concern of the clever personality is not the accomplishment of the work in the most complete way, but mere success in achieving the goal lest he be called incapable or incompetent. For what matters to him most is that he perform the task in a way that maintains his personal façade.

The clever student in our milieus is the one who always succeeds without exerting himself in the toil of constant serious studying, bragging about that and disparaging the miserable secluded colleague who spends night and day going over his class lessons. He reproaches him with various affronts like "the rote learner," "he who memorizes but does not understand what he is reading," or "a brute of studying and learning." The clever student concerns himself, first and last, with apparent success and the external appearance that comes with this success, and thus we see him seeking refuge in every trick and illicit method to obtain success, including flattering the teacher (and sometimes bribing him), cheating in examinations, and breaking his head speculating as to which questions he will be required to answer in the examination. His eternal dream is that a copy of the exam questions falls into his hands before the exam. We all are familiar with the rest of the story since we were students or our children today are students.

What is painful in this matter is that most of us approach this type of behavior as if it were a natural matter and without a pang

---

1   *Fi Bina' al-Bashar: Dirasat fi'l-Tagyir al-Hadari wa'l-Fikr al-Tarbawi* [*On Building Human Beings: Studies in Cultural Change and Educational Thought*] (Sirsa Liyan: Center for Social Development in the Arab World, 1964), 80–91.

of conscience, self-examination, or internal resistance saying to ourselves, "your success is false, hollow, and empty, without validity or authority." What scares us is not the failure in itself, but the shame and disgrace that we believe descends on us when the news of our failure spreads and becomes known. How many college students have I known who concealed the news of their failure from their family and friends even if they deserved to fail and boast of their success in front of them even if they did not deserve it since they gained it in a crooked, illicit way? As for the calamity, that is when this clever student advances from behind the school desk and becomes an officer in the army or an important official in the state administration, bringing along with him the pattern of his clever behavior, applying it automatically and innocently to his present work. What happens to us when this clever officer tries to find the shortest route, whatever it is, so that it is said that he is a successful officer and thus spares himself what he considers disgraceful and shameful, that he acknowledges failure and tries to overcome it? What happens to the nation when this officer does well in his military tours and rises from rank to rank with ways and means that resemble those he practiced to ascend through school and obtain a secondary school or university diploma, for example? What happens to the nation when this clever officer flatters his superiors in the most important matters and explains to them that he has mastered information and studies that he, in truth, knows little of, exactly as he flattered his professors in the university and pretended to have mastered the details of his studies while he, in truth, copied from his colleagues or from a paper he sneaked into the examination hall?

This traditional tendency of the clever personality towards hiding defects and maintaining an appearance in front of others that is at odds with the reality of our situation (behaving according to the Sunna, "If you are afflicted with sins, hide") is what lends special importance to what President Abdel Nasser said in the speech he gave on one of the military bases:

> And then, at the same time, if we conceal our failings now they will just reappear during the battle. Each commander must admit the failings around him. I was very happy when I saw

the division commander and he informed me what were the failings and shortcomings about him. This is a new approach. If we conceal our failings today, how will we remedy them.[1]

It is clear from the sense of this speech that this tendency of the clever personality is as widespread in the ranks of the military forces as it is in traditional Arab society as a whole, and that effectively fighting it is a new course of action that started after the defeat, just as President Abdel Nasser mentioned.

These traditional traits of the clever personality render us unable to accept reality and the truth, in compliance with what critical circumstances impose in terms of speedy action, and force us to conceal our faults, failures, and shortcomings in order to maintain appearances and save face. This concealment is clearly exemplified in Heikal's referring to "some faults of behavior" that appeared in the Arab military personnel on the morning of the attack on the United Arab Republic's air bases. In revealing some of what was hidden concerning the massacre that the Arab air force was exposed to in Egypt, Heikal said the following:

> The Israeli calculation relied on some faults of behavior caused by a lack of discipline, the fault of tardiness in communicating unfavorable truths to the higher levels. This fault gave the enemy the ten minutes it precisely needed in order to achieve surprise in the eleven bases it targeted in its first strike...the first raid was on some more exposed airbases in the Sinai, but faults in behavior played their role in slowing the speed of communication and losing priceless minutes, etc. The reliance of the Israeli deed on this particular behavioral fault is not the inference or personal judgment of anyone, but how the head of the Israeli air force, Mordechai Hud, explained the timing of his plan.[2]

Naturally, General Hud did not compose the timing of the plan solely on the basis of a simple fault of behavior, as Heikal suggests in

---

1   *Al-Anwar*, Beirut (April 30, 1968).
2   *Al-Ahram* (June 28, 1968).

accordance with good manners, good breeding, and the preservation of appearances. He composed the plan on the basis of a precise understanding of the characteristics of the traditional model of inherited Arab life and a precise appraisal of the nature of the patterns of behavior and the reactions that individuals acquire in the likes of this traditional society, and the types of priorities that were planted in their psyche as the values of shame, concealing faults, and hiding unfavorable truths. The qualities that Heikal discusses are not just simple faults but rather enormous residues, and even mountains that weigh on the shoulders of the Arab who attempts to adapt himself to the new forms of life and battle.

The Revolution should have been fully aware of the disadvantages these ancient remnants impose on the Arab citizen in general and the Arab soldier in particular. It should have worked hard to uproot and overcome all of them by means of schools and the education of a new revolutionary generation, on the one hand, and by means of hard, vigorous training and a modern socialist education of the military ranks, on the other. For there is nothing in these remnants and in the traits of the *fahlawi* personality that render them impossible to overcome and uproot if we are ready to make the required effort and offer the necessary sacrifices. There can be no deep and long-lasting socialist revolution unless the formation of its citizens, its young, and its successive generations has the highest priority.

One of the characteristics of the clever personality that Dr. 'Ammar mentions is its tendency to sudden enthusiasm, extreme boldness, and scoffing at difficulties at the beginning of the road, then indifference and apathy when the clever personality surmises that the matter calls for steadfastness, perseverance, and systematic action, and that the results will only emerge slowly and cumulatively. Who of us does not recognize that alert Arab youth who rushed out during the heat of battle seeking weapons and wishing that he were only able to pilot a war plane or drive an armored vehicle, although he probably had never carried anything other than a hunting rifle? However, he is ready to sacrifice himself for the cause.

Let us leave the battlefront and return with this youth to the region of daily life and its routines. He is an employee in one of the state offices, working six hours a day, from eight in the morning until two in the afternoon, and after lunch he enjoys a period of napping, and then he plays cards or backgammon and talks politics in his favorite café, afterwards catching some television or relaxing in some way in the evening in order to return to the same routine on the following day. Let us attempt now to make him understand that the weekly hours of work will increase to nine hours a day because of the necessity of building the country in accordance with the new socialist plan, or that he must from now on persevere in his office past noon to complete the tasks that are piling up. Try to demand from him that he maintains more punctuality in appointments, that you expect from him a discernible increase in activity and production, or that you expect from him that he take some responsibilities for his individual activities and personal initiatives. Try to convince him to change his well-known routine of life since he fritters away most of his daylight hours, including a part of his official work hours, and try also to convince him that he busy himself during his long free hours with something useful and profitable. How will this youth react? Rejection, reluctance, pretext, and secret attempts to escape from making the exertion required to exit from the circle of his empty routine and hollow monotony. He is, simply said, like the clever student who cannot make the connection between changing the manner of doing his work, the routines of his life, his behavior, and his social relationships, on the one hand, and the battle that he wants to join with such enthusiasm, on the other. He is not yet aware of his duty in adapting to the new conditions necessary for achieving victory, and that his clinging to this pattern of life hinders the advancement of the country and the achieving of the goal that he was ready to die for in the hour of enthusiasm and zeal, because this clinging is reaction and sluggishness themselves. Just as he does not realize that the new obligations that the socialist transformation imposes on the pattern of his daily life, and especially in the execution of the tasks for which he is directly responsible, parallels in importance his immediate but temporary zeal to carry arms when war breaks out. The solution to these problems does not end with raising consciousness or giving advice and guidance, but passes over to radical changes in the character of the social and educational institutions that rear these youths and establish a large part of their *fahlawi* and backward way of life, wasting human, mental, and productive capacities.

In reality, this is a chief difficulty that the committed revolutionary Arab youth suffers under, since his revolution, most of the time, is nothing more than a revolution at the political level. In other words, it does not reach deeper than superstructures and does not disturb operatively and actively the level of social relationships and how its traditional fabric stamps its sluggish backward imprint on the primary level. For in spite of his revolution at the political level, we keep finding that his social relationships, family ties, judgments in matters public and private, and general behavior towards his work and immediate surroundings all spring from the values, modes of behavior, and reactionary judgments of traditional society that he was supposed to have rejected since he considers himself in revolt against it.

In other words, the Arab revolutionary youth today is a political revolutionary but, in the depths of his heart, he is usually a social, religious, cultural, ethical, and economic conservative. His claim to differ on the theoretical level does not prove anything because revolutionary theory has no positive impact unless it is transformed into new modes of behavior that the revolutionary person practices in his surroundings instinctively, and out of which he makes a new positive factor in his society and environment. Similarly, close contact with individuals and groups of Arab youth who consider themselves revolutionary always astonishes me since as soon as their talk departs from political topics (fighting the Zionists, resisting colonialism, etc.), I observe an abrupt and radical transformation: their opinions, actions, judgments, values, and modes of behavior concerning all matters of life and society are like a slightly revised and enlightened miniature of the behavior, opinions, and values of our fathers, our mothers, and even our grandparents. Such youths are supposed to be opposed to these values, since they are supposed to be progressive revolutionaries. For if they are not in revolt against the dark image of the past, and progressive compared to their predecessors, then what are they revolting against, and whom are they more progressive than? Unless the revolutionary position is comprehensive and inclusive of the revolutionary's personality, deeds, ties, viewpoints, and sensibilities, all molded anew in an integrated and novel way, it remains fragmentary, superficial, and ineffective.

In other words, the revolutionary attitude in the revolutionary person ought to manifest itself in a new transformation and new viewpoint that makes its mark not only at the political level but also at the level of routine matters in our lives that we have become accustomed to accept without discussion or revision because of their entrenchment and our long close contact with them. In this sense, the revolutionary attitude passes beyond politics to include a concrete practical and radical position that emerges daily in the behavior of the revolutionary in the course of his interaction with culture, training, and education, the university and its faculties, the family and the specific character of his ties to it, the harsh patriarchal foundation of traditional societies, women in society, and his private life, etc. For either he exhibits revolutionary behavior in regards to these institutions by a rejection of their obsolete, inherited form as a first step or he remains at a shallow, superficial level in his revolt. We do no injustice if we say that revolutionary Arab youths (male or female) who have begun to behave in a revolutionary manner spontaneously and automatically in regards to the matters of life that we have given as examples are truly rare, for they are, in fact, very conservative, as I mentioned.[1]

---

1   Lenin devoted special attention to this phenomenon among revolutionaries (especially the committed youth among them), writing numerous analyses and criticizing it with biting and intense scorn. If the comrades whose superficial revolutionary commitment Lenin scorned were excused twenty years into this century, what is the excuse of the youths who consider themselves revolutionaries and to be committed to the same goals with only thirty years to go in this century? What follows is a section from the discussion Lenin held with Clara Zetkin in which he treated the phenomenon of a superficial revolutionary commitment among the comrades with criticism, scorn, and mockery, as appears with clarity in a very clearly-defined and sensitive issue, the attitude of the revolutionary man towards women and their traditional place in society.

Lenin said: "Unfortunately, we can still say of many of our communist comrades that 'if you scratch the skin of one of them, superficiality and pettiness appear underneath.' You must, of course, scratch sensitive spots like their mentality in regards to women. Is there a more tangible proof than the familiar sight of the man observing with complete calm a woman wasting herself with petty, routine activities like household work, depleting her time and strength: He watches her vitality disappear, her mind grow stupid, the beating of her heart slacken, and her will weaken. Of course, I do not need to say that I am not speaking of the bourgeois ladies who cast the burden of household labor and the toil of children entirely on

According to the analysis of Dr. 'Ammar, the clever personality is characterized by other traits, like the exaggeration of self-assurance and the persistent tendency to advertise superior power in the control of affairs. Similarly, it appears in the behavior of individuals who are generous with their promises, when they say, for example, "Consider the problem solved, I have influence with the minister," "Whatever you want, leave it to me, and I guarantee it," "All set, take it from me," and the rest of these widespread, well-known expressions. Among the manifestations of the self-assurance of the clever personality are despising the other, devaluing him, and affecting a superior prowess in solving problems. This is clear from the behavior of those who assert themselves and boast of their superiority by scoffing and mocking others without their knowing that they have fallen prey to the pranks of the clever personality.

In every group of people there is someone who is distinguished by that he "confuses the people" or "pulls a prank on the other" or "ridicules" everyone, as we say in our colloquial speech. Thus we find that if someone shows a greater interest in his work than is usual among his colleagues, or offers new ideas about how to achieve the goal of work and calls for their implementation, or is intent on a sound application of rules, regulations and principles

---

servants. My words apply to the overwhelming majority of women, among them even the wives of workers who pass their days in factories making money.

Few are the husbands, even among the ranks of the proletariat, whom it strikes to what extent they are able to relieve the weight of the burdens and troubles cast on the shoulders of their wives if they lent a hand in completing 'this women's work.' Naturally, they do not make this effort since it would be at odds with the 'prerogatives' of the husband and 'his dignity,' this husband who insists always on ensuring rest for himself. The home life of the women is a daily self-sacrifice to a thousand and one trivialities. The ancient rights of her husband – 'her master and lord' – still continue in effect, concealed and unobserved. However, this slave of his has a secret influence on him in an objective aspect, since the reality of her backwardness and absence of engrossment in his revolutionary ideals undermine his fighting resolution and impede his determination to fight...I know the life of the worker, and my knowledge is not from books alone. Our communist work among the masses of women and our general political work both include a great deal of educational work among the men. We must root out from the party and from among the masses this ancient view of women, the view of the slave-master of his slaves. This is one of our political duties, and it is an urgent and necessary one, like our urgent duties in forming organizations of comrades, men and women, well trained in theory and practice, to carry on party work among working women."

to perfect the work in the hope that it emerges as a model or in an ideal form, he is often the butt of sarcasm and mocking from his clever colleagues who describe him as a "puritan," a "true believer" or as "someone who has risen above his station."[1]

I have no doubt that the characteristics of "cleverness" in despising the other, on the one hand, and self-assertion on a negative basis, on the other, were, to a great extent, the source of what I mentioned in the beginning of this account about the Arab tendency before the war (and even after it) to scorn the prowess and capabilities of the enemy and to take him lightly, and reassure ourselves, this self that lacks deep confidence in itself, by way of resounding pretensions and an attachment to external appearances and forms. Thus we treat the possession of MIG planes like the possession of strings of blue beads that will protect us from the evil staring down at us.

The clever personality nurses real feelings of inferiority and is not able to admit them because it clings to the values of shame and fear of scandal more than it clings to realism, objectivity, and the necessity of frankly acknowledging its inferiority in order to treat and overcome it.

Likewise, we see it excel in superficial appeasements and transient civility whose aim is to hide the real situation and conceal the true feelings just as in our everyday expressions, "never mind," "it's simple," "everything is okay" and "we are all brothers." We all know to what extent the relations among the Arab states are usually characterized by this superficial appeasement and transient civility whose end is concealing the circumstances as they really are, and this description suits, in particular, the relationships between the Arab states before the war, and even after it.

Similarly, the clever personality is ill at ease doing voluntary collective work. The source of its discomfort is that it might be exposed to sensitive situations in which it lacks competence and that it fears the exposure of its weaknesses, contrary to the appearance it prefers to maintain. If there is no escape from working in common, this work loses everything associated with "team spirit" and loses too the individual's knowledge of how to fulfill his role

---

1   'Asam al-Din Hawas, *Thawrat al-Akhlaq* [*Revolution of Character*] (Cairo: 1967).

in the group and perform in harmony with others to complete the common task. It is clear that relations among the Arab states (when they have to voluntarily work together) are characterized, to a great extent, by "apparent agreement," "mere going along with the others," "appeasement of each other" and "brotherhood," but without genuine commitment to any collective responsibilities and to what these impose. These relations carry, as well, all the traits and sensitivities of the clever personality described above.

When the clever personality finds itself in a tight jam that will necessarily expose its weakness and deficiencies, it excels in shifting responsibility away from itself and projecting it on external forces, thus enabling it to explain away the negative results it has produced. Just as the clever Arab student does not blame himself for failing the exam but blames instead luck, the professor, the difficult questions, the government, the regime, or the divine, so the nation blames the enemy, colonialism, deception, luck, and everything that occurs to it, thus making it easy on itself, saving face, protecting appearances, sparing feelings, and raising morale instead of penetrating to the origin of the disease and extirpating it. In a similar way, we observed earlier in this study how the Arab acknowledgment of responsibility for the consequences of the 5th of June came both late and couched in a careful, wary, reluctant language that did not surpass the level of generalities that do not puncture or disturb traditional proprieties.

It is also apparent that the clever personality is strongly committed to the concepts of chivalry, masculinity, nobility, honor, boldness, and courage that I mentioned earlier. Since the clever personality thrives in societies that model their behavior and views on traditional modes of life where the perceptions, ideas, and reactions of individuals are turned towards deep-rooted habits and inherited ancestral customs, making the individual in these societies a person conservative in body and mind who always operates within a defined, established orbit, the venerable is left standing and protected in order that it be passed onto the next generation. Likewise, this individual is characterized by the sluggishness that pervades the rhythm of life in his surroundings, and, because of his education and upbringing, he does not embark on stepping beyond the past, going beyond its realities, or devising new solutions for its old problems. In other words, he always prefers to take the conventional path and withdraw to the ready-made structures in which he is at home. Accordingly, we see that this society favors the old over the young and tribal elders over youth, disregarding the competencies that each possesses, as if merely staying alive was the only measure of a person, or bestows certain rights regardless of accomplishments or achievements. The June War exposed a great number of people in sensitive military, scientific, and technical positions whose sole sufficient capital and justification for remaining was the passing of time, respect for years, status, seniority, and rank, while such posts should have been occupied by personalities that value in their work nothing but positive results, i.e., competence and tangible production.

I mention these matters because the qualities of sluggishness, the inclination for tradition, the clinging and sticking to ready structures, and the shunning of rapid improvisation and direct initiative in making decisions have left very dangerous negative effects in our military organizations and on how we think about modern war, and they are responsible to a great extent for the rapid defeat that descended upon us. No doubt that all of those following the news of the war in detail and with some objectivity have discovered that one of the most significant weaknesses of the Arab army in the Sinai was its inability to maneuver quickly and move without interruption in order to conform promptly to the developments of the battle being fought. Israel applied a strategy of Blitzkrieg that depended on absolute freedom of movement, as it is known in wars of the desert and plains. President Abdel Nasser pointed to this fact in one of his speeches where he mentioned "that the Israelis applied the principle of surprise war, and then of nimbleness, and then of flexibility, and then of the concentration of forces." Then he added, "By applying these four principles they were able to win the Six-Day War. [1] As for our troops in the Sinai, they were in the thrall of the traditional conservative mentality, and thus they fought with a fortifications mentality and a strategy of static resistance. As long as the enemy was attacking their positions directly and face to face they defended them fearlessly and with great courage, but as

---

1   *Al-Anwar* (Beirut: April 30, 1968)

soon as the enemy had recourse to some deceptions and tricks that depended on quick movement and nimble maneuvers, it punctured the Arab defensive positions without great strain, and it appears that much of the war was nothing but a series of mobile maneuvers that the enemy army established as traps for our soldiers, and which they fell into almost without exception.

The following section from a speech of President Abdel Nasser clarifies the reality of the Arab conception of war as traditional direct confrontation lacking the distinguishing features of dynamism demanded by modern war (note the emphasis and persistent insistence of Abdel Nasser on the idea of face-to-face confrontation), saying:

> Our armed forces did not confront the Israelis face to face as a whole in the battle of last June. A fraction of our armed forces confronted the Israeli forces, but the greater part did not confront the Israeli forces face to face. The fraction that confronted the Israeli forces fought with courage and valor and inflicted grave losses on the enemy. No one can deny that in the battles involving face-to-face confrontation, people defied death, died, and inflicted many losses on the enemy.[1]

The same chivalric model of Arab thinking about the fighting emerges in a boast by the Jordanian prime minister during the war concerning the boldness of the Jordanian soldier (and no one at all denies the courage of the Arab fighters in general) where he says about the Israelis: "They know, from before and after, how the Jordanian soldier fights when there is a confrontation between soldiers, not between soldiers and fire directed down on them from the sky."[2] What good comes from this boast if the nature of war has changed and it no longer depends on confrontations between soldiers, but rather on fire that is aimed from the sky? So either we confront this fire with fire like it or we defuse the effect of its superiority by using the strategy of a war of liberation that rejects

---

1 Ibid.
2 Sa`d Jum`ah, *Al-Mu'amarah wa Ma'rakat al-Masir* [*The Conspiracy and the Battle of Destiny*] (Beirut: 1967), 196.

entirely the idea of a direct confrontation with the enemy. As for merely boasting of chivalric courage, there is nothing to be gained and no advantage to be hoped for except in consolation.

Another example of what I am saying is the Arab armored vehicles buried in deep ditches in the sand in order to use their powerful guns from behind defensive fortifications. However, burying armored vehicles in this way robs them of their most salient characteristic, the ability to move and maneuver. In other words, we adhered during this war to the greatest extent to the pattern of our life, a pattern that still essentially employs tradition and custom rather than dynamism, mobility, and ingenuity. Thus we entrenched ourselves in fortified positions out of fear of a mobile and fluid war, in spite of the fact that we had previously boasted of how quickly and competently our forces could move from place to place. In other words, we, as usual, bragged about appearance and form, and, like the clever personality, abandoned the kernel and core.

In reality, the traditional Arab clinging to formalities, proprieties, appearances, and established routine was so intense that the Arab leaders and fighters could not overcome and free themselves from it even in the most urgent and pressing moments. What follows is an incident described by Heikal in one his articles that gives us the most eloquent example of what I am saying. Heikal mentions (*Al-Ahram*, June 28, 1968) that Field Marshall 'Abd al-Hakim 'Amir boarded a warplane at eight o'clock on the morning of the 5th of June 1967 heading to one of the airbases in Sinai, where most of the front commanders were "standing waiting for him in the arrival section of the airbase, far from their command centers, conforming to socially and militarily-backward fusty traditional protocols – even in time of war." As for the rest, we know how it turned out.

Among the negative aspects of this traditionalism and conservativism that reflected itself on the course of the war was the inability of the officers who were directly supervising the military operations in the Sinai to accept the responsibility for taking swift, immediate decisions based on the development of the battle from hour to hour without constantly going back to the higher leadership in order to receive orders that detailed everything no matter how minor. In fact, the initiative in taking resolute decisions according to what the immediate, constantly changing battlefield circumstances imposes during the battle and adapting to them was largely lost. In other words, the Arab officers during the battle applied ready-made strategic and tactical frameworks while the enemy did the complete opposite, and the Arab militaries were unable to depart from their pre-set strategic models by resorting to initiative and improvisation in order to confront the enemy as they had to confront him, regardless of the original order of battle. Régis Debray describes this problem by saying:

> But the force of tradition, the deep-rooted adherence to forms of organization fixed and hallowed by time, prevents the dissolution of an established structure and the passage to a new form of struggle required by the war situation.[1]

The blame for this failure does not fall on the officers as individuals alone, since the mentalities of "we have no orders" and "we have no instructions," that is, the fear of bearing responsibility for acting or not acting without previous permission from our rulers does not only appear in the battlefield. They are, in fact, a basic part of the fabric of Arab society, customs, and character, and it is this society that forms and produces these officers. These officers grew up in a traditional society, probably in conservative families that submit to the father's authority in all matters big and small, that demand their constant obedience to those older, higher in rank, and greater in status, restrict them to what is well-known, usual, and familiar, and deny them the chance to practice the right of choice in the important matters in their life (including marriage). So how can they learn the meaning of the responsibility that follows from the act of choice and individual initiative? For it is not assumed in this dominant social system that they practice these sorts of actions, decisions, and choices, and bear responsibility for them, except after they are heads of families or in high leadership positions. Likewise, it appears to me to be hopeless to expect from our officers in the hell of war flexible behavior, swift individual initiative, and taking responsibility for final decisions without going back to those who are their superiors in age, rank, or status after we have raised them

---

1 Régis Debray, *Revolution in the Revolution* (London: Penguin Books, 1968) 72.

in a way that runs in the entirely opposite direction to the models of behavior, values, and reactions that a war of unrestricted movement and a modern desert war impose. Either our society emerges from its shell with a strength and fervor it has yet to know in order to face these challenges or it accepts defeat and withdraws to the rear.

Everything I mentioned about the well-known mentality of "we have no orders" and "we have no instructions" goes no further than being a description of the painful reality that has not changed since the first Arab-Israeli war, despite all the arms that we have imported, the political shakeups that we have passed through, and the revolutionary regimes that we have witnessed. When war broke out, it turned out that the first mentality truly dominated the reactions of the Arab fighters, evidence for which is what Heikal mentioned about the behavior demonstrated by the defense batteries positioned at the air bases in the United Arab Republic, who did not open anti-aircraft fire against the planes of the enemy (as the bombs were falling down on them) because they were awaiting orders and directives! Heikal stated:

> The defense batteries at the airbases found the enemy above them actively dropping bombs...They had to await the order to begin firing at the enemy, although this appears now to be complete madness, but the traditional centralization imposed it in a moment of greatest urgency and danger. (*Al-Ahram*, June 28, 1968.)

IV

I must broach an important topic that is a center of fierce discussion in some Arab newspapers and magazines: the call to adopt the Vietnamese paradigm in the struggle against Israel and colonialism. In regards to this paradigm of liberating the country, we find a people about whom it is said that they are poor, backward, and isolated, but who resisted French colonialism with fierceness and remarkable acts of heroism. Today this people faces the greatest military power in the world, with its planes, napalm, and the most modern weapons. Let us imitate it and follow its path in the popular war of liberation. We must recognize in this matter, first, that victorious popular wars of liberation, unlike the mere resisting of occupation, do not come instantly and on the basis of a hasty call to pursue them after the organized army of the country suffered defeat, but rather as a result of the anticipation that it will be a popular war of liberation from its beginning to its end. In other words, it does not typically spring from the desire to instantly replace what the people have lost in the defeat of their traditional military, for if it springs from the likes of this conception it will, most of the time, be emaciated and incomplete in its effectiveness and results, and closer to an adventure than to a bold revolutionary action. The popular war of liberation has both its own nature and rules and regulations, and it cannot be conjured up as a hasty substitute for the failure of the traditional organized military apparatus or sought as a second line of defense after the failure of the first line of defense.

As long as the Arabs have no alternative except to adopt the method of the popular war of liberation, they must adopt it as an autonomous reality, not as a measure we are forced to adopt because we did not know how to win with the military measures we had preferred to it, and that we still prefer to it at the official level at least. The important thing is for the Arab popular war of liberation to come into being and, after that, it will impose itself on the reluctant leadership by the degree of its use of force and its practical success.

Second, it goes without saying that experiences of armed popular struggle do not transfer automatically from one country to another or from region to region, but each popular movement leading this sort of struggle must develop the methods that suit it, in light of the experience of others, to confront the invading and occupying enemy. Even now we are not able to predict the specific character of the methods that the Arab struggle will develop, if it finally decides to enter the battle wholeheartedly by means of the popular war of liberation. The Arab struggle for the liberation of Palestine must develop its particular methods because the methods of the Vietnamese struggle are not applicable as a whole and in detail to our battle with the enemy.

For the Arab fedayeen are not able to sneak into Tel Aviv or Haifa as the Vietnamese militants are able to enter Saigon in great numbers and then stay there for shorter or longer periods among the people and inhabitants, according to the demands of the military operation. If the Arab fedayeen stay among the inhabitants of the West Bank, for example, then their effectiveness becomes limited, since Israel has no important installations to attack in the West Bank, and thus its scope of action is confined to attacking military patrols and blowing up equipment.

Third, it appears to me that Vietnam has largely succeeded in overcoming its underdevelopment and, especially, the models of apathetic, sluggish, traditional behavior that always accompany the fact of underdevelopment in some countries. For since the state of socialist Vietnam was established, it has firmly adhered to Lenin's directive to socialism: "Socialism is the rule of the Soviets plus the electrification of the country." In other words, the program of basic industry and modernizing the means of production have not ceased in socialist Vietnam even in the most extreme conditions of war and aerial bombing. The Vietnamese guerilla has entirely perfected what the Arab soldier failed to implement on the 5th of June, the war of constant, uninterrupted movement, the war of flexibility, initiative, and quick, bold, direct decisions, the war of swift reactions that seizes the simplest opportunity and transforms it to the advantage of the struggle against the colonialist enemy, and that guides the conflict with a scientific mentality that truly knows how to create from the most negligible material deadly, effective weapons against the enemy, and transform the abundant raw materials, no matter what kind, to resources that strengthen the ability of the fighters to destroy the enemy and continue fighting.

The mentality that is able to create with such skill, organize with such precision, and extract latent human and natural powers and turn them into effective force has, without doubt or suspicion, stepped beyond the stage of underdevelopment. The success of the Vietnamese struggle has its source, to a great extent, in the level of planning and implementation possessed by the Vietnamese systems, in its quality of leadership, and in its political and social organizations. All of this functions at a very high level of coordination, planning, experience, and sophistication to extract all the latent powers of the people and drive its human resources into the service of the struggle for liberation.

There is nothing more indicative of this than the concentrated assault that the Vietnamese fighters undertook at the beginning of the lunar year across and along the whole country, this assault on all the enemy positions at one time, unprecedented in the history of wars of liberation in regards to its precision, organization, effectiveness, coordination, and boldness, as the American enemy itself has acknowledged. Under the supervision of this leadership, the state of war in Vietnam was transformed into an opportunity and tool to achieve social, organizational, and revolutionary changes in the life of the Vietnamese people, the undertaking of which in a radical manner would have been impractical in normal circumstances. In all fairness, one should not make prejudgments on the course of the armed Arab resistance to the Israeli occupation or speak of it in a decisive, final manner because previous experiences have taught us that these events are subject to mutations and eruptions that lend them a strength and capacity that could not be calculated or predicted beforehand. Therefore, the intensification of the work of the Palestinian fedayeen in the occupied territories remains the advance front in the battle for liberation. However, in order for the action of the Arab fedayeen to transcend the stage of fedayeen action and enter the stage of the popular war of liberation, the Arab states surrounding Palestine must draw the enemy into a protracted war, in which the Arabs will be hit hard and make sacrifices without appealing for help or surrendering until the strength and concentrated power of the enemy are gradually depleted.

The basic problem, then, does not lie in the transformation of the occupied territory into South Vietnam, but in the extent of our readiness to transform the Arab states adjacent to Palestine into North Vietnam on every level, since the popular war of liberation requires, in addition to truly effective popular political and partisan organizations, bases for supply, attack, and retreat to be provided by the Arab states directly concerned with the fight for the liberation of Palestine. However, we must admit and acknowledge, with all regrets, that the idea of popular liberation until today has not met with an active response or strong acceptance as the surest means to confront Israel in the Arab east. It appears that the Arabs in general, including the most progressive Arab regimes, do not truly favor taking the necessary steps to begin a popular war of liberation and draw the enemy into its battles. The military preparations to repair what proved flawed after the war in our military force runs in the direction of rebuilding the Arab military force according to the model of an organized army with conventional weapons. In relation to the military role that popular organizations can play, only the concept of popular resistance draws any attention today. However, a popular war of liberation cannot rely merely on resistance, but requires total adherence to continuous offensive tactics that take the battle to the enemy according to its, not the enemy's, advantage. I will return to discuss some of these vital matters pertaining to the question of the popular war of liberation and its connection to other aspects of the life of society in the rest of the study.

V

Much was said before and, especially, after the defeat about the importance of modern science, scientific research, and technological application in relation to Arab society, and in relation to the more advanced and progressive Arab states, both as a vital necessity in confronting the Israeli challenges in particular and the challenges of modern industrial society in general. Heikal's declaration has been cited: "The Arab side has no other solution at the line of total confrontation than that it be educated and modern." Everyone knows that President Abdel Nasser laid stress in most of his speeches after the defeat on the topic of science and technology, as occurred, for example, in the remarks that he gave in one of his visits to the military positions along the battlefront:

> Today war has become a scientific war before it is anything else. We cannot achieve this superiority except on the foundation of the total absorption of science and technology.

You as leaders are in need of science and technology. We, for our part, strive to obtain the most modern weapons. I have arranged that Soviet experts come so that we can learn from them the secrets and methods of using the weapons that we have obtained from the Soviet Union. Our enemies have been undergoing technological training for years and they have exceptional information. They apply what they have learned. If we lack an exceptional level of training and knowledge of science and technology, then we will not be capable of applying what is in the book. Thus, we must absorb information and knowledge.[1]

This is an essential and important speech, and it assumes that the revolutionary Arab leaders should have recognized the importance of its message from the time they tossed around their socialist slogans, since socialism cannot be built without the total adoption and complete embrace of modern science and its institutions, applications, and programs. Thus we can infer the level of neglect that beset our institutions, down to its fundaments, from the declarations of the Arab rulers and leaders themselves. As an example, let us examine some statements made by the current war minister in the United Arab Republic, Fariq Awal Fawzi, who said in a speech:

One of the lessons we learned from this battle is the importance of raising the skill, capability, and effectiveness of the fighting soldier...It has become imperative that the fighting soldier be an individual with a particular cultural level...One of the conclusions that we drew from the previous battle is the inability of the illiterate soldier to understand the method of battle...Why do we select the illiterate when he is unsuited for the requirements of modern equipment? This is why priority in joining the armed forces is given to the educated and cultured, and this made many things available to us. For if there are enough men, why not choose the better? Here the better means ranking in learning and education, since the one we seek will be at home as an individual with the intricacies of

---

1   *Al-Nahar*, March 13, 1968.

modern weapons. All initiative in the armed forces, whether in training, planning, or the understanding of operations, is built on scientific foundations.[1]

Was the defeat of the 5th of June truly necessary in order that the Arab leaders, and especially the revolutionaries among them, recognize these simple axioms about "the inability of the illiterate man to understand the method of battle," his inability to interact with sophisticated weapons, and the necessity to choose the better man for the appropriate position? Did we regard modern science as another slogan tossed about without realizing what the scientific mentality entails at the level of daily practice and constant, effective, cumulative application? Dr. Sameer Hanna summarizes the Arab attitude towards modern science in the following way:

> Whenever we appraise the lessons of the setback, and draw from them our understandings, we must remember that the most important of these lessons is that we neglected science in the past years. We regarded it and treated it entirely as the rural mayor regards a modern irrigating machine that he bought.
>
> He shows it to his guests, talks about its magical power, and boasts about what he paid for it, but he never operates it except on special occasions, usually falling back on the water wheel and "shadoof" to irrigate his fields.

Dr. Hanna then calls on the leaders of the United Arab Republic to take the necessary steps to formulate sound revolutionary principles to overcome the phenomenon of scientific underdevelopment, emphasizing that every socialist country in the world skimps on food in order to invest in its universities. The neglect of the universities is one of the signs of underdevelopment, and, within the context of our system, it is one of the signs of reactionary thinking.[2]

---

1   *Al-Anwar*, April 11, 1968, 5.
2   *Al-Katib* [*The Writer*] magazine (Cairo: August, 1967).

We must not remain at the level of abstraction, universals, and generalities in discussing the subject of modern science in relation to Arab society, but must introduce some details and particulars in order that our critique proves beneficial. However, before I record my observations about these details, I must make clear to the reader that I, in my discussion of the scope of the effectiveness of the scientific mentality and its achievements in Arab society (and especially in the more progressive Arab societies), am not proposing to delay the direct struggle against the occupation or the battle for liberation with the Zionists until we triumph over our technical and scientific underdevelopment. In reality, we are with those who believe that the struggle for a strong, scientific, and modern socialist Arab society is tightly, directly, and organically bound with the Arab battle against the Zionists and its imperialist supporters. The Arab revolutionary regimes are able today – if they want – to profit from the lessons of the defeat and the existing state of war to serve the goals of social, socialist, and scientific development in the Arab nation (or some part of it, at least), and to extend its elements, thoughts, and values deeper into the Arab consciousness and mind. Similarly, they are able to transform the present crisis into an opportunity to achieve revolutionary social, economic, and organizational changes in society that strengthen and deepen the roots of scientific socialism in Arab life. Every step in this direction forms in itself an intensification in the battle against Zionists and colonialist powers, pushing it forward. There are numerous examples of peoples that have waded into fierce, liberating, patriotic battles against the colonialists while they were building industry, socialism, and progress at the same time, and we have mentioned some of them. Until we learn from these examples and make use of them at the level of daily work and effective practice, we will not succeed in confronting the deadly challenges around us at the radical level required.

Some of the commentators on the Arab circumstances after the defeat (and especially the progressives among them) seem to presume that a discussion of the defeat from the point of view of the prevailing scientific level in some particular Arab countries, for example, and on the basis of the question of modernity and the renewal of the means of production and social relationships in their comprehensive meanings is nothing but flight from the confrontation of the occupation and the battle for liberation by means of a popular war of liberation.[1] Their evidence is the current fact that raising the level of the Arab nation in terms of science and production and its transformation to a modern society, etc. forms a long process absorbing generations, while the present occupation of Arab land cannot endure such a delay. I do not doubt that the liberal Arab circles calling for a modern Arab society want to make from the call for the triumph over underdevelopment a substitute for the only Arab response with guaranteed results against the expansionist Zionist presence on Arab lands, namely, a popular war of liberation. However, the basic error in this pattern of thinking is stating the case in such a way as to create an apparent conflict between the striving of the nation and its revolutionary leadership in hope of overcoming underdevelopment and advancing towards a modern society, on the one hand, and the method of the popular war of liberation (with what it requires in the way of a mobilization and organization of the popular masses) in confronting the enemy, on the other hand. The incompatibility between these two goals is nothing but a delusion, since the great masters of the popular war of liberation in this century have never passed up an opportunity to insist – at the level of theory and practice – that the consequences of a war of liberation are the shaking of the traditional fabric of social life and the striking at its various indifferent, lazy, and sluggish relationships, customs, and values, which are inimical and obstructive to the process of modernization itself. That is, the war of liberation – in the view of its leaders and their experiences – facilitates the process of modernization, accelerates it in an unparalleled manner, and radically levels the path to the building of a modern, scientifically socialist society after the end of the war. The significance of the popular war of liberation is not latent in only its "negative" consequences, like the driving out of the occupation and the emancipation from the hegemony of the colonizer entirely, but also in its positive consequences, since the

---

1   For an example, see the article of Mohammed Kashlee in the magazine *Al-Hurriya* [*Freedom*] (Beirut: August 7, 1967).

direct or indirect participation of the individual in the resistance or popular military efforts leads by necessity to the widening of that individual's horizons so that he comprehends the existence of his country and nation, not merely that of his tribe and family. It also creates in the individual a sense of his integral importance in the national effort and the building of the nation, and strengthens in him the values of discipline, reliability, and the appreciation of work, time, and the rest of the general and necessary considerations for the process of modernization and building a modern socialist state.[1]

The revolutionary fighters in Vietnam were able to solve the difficult equation of defusing American scientific and technological superiority and neutralizing it to their advantage with an analogous scientific mind that attained – by means of their popular political, fighting, and military experiences – a level of scientific progress in planning, inventing, organizing, and precision in implementation that no popular revolution had achieved before. The Arabs have never approached this attainment despite all the heavy modern munitions and sensitive precise equipment that they have accumulated in their weapons storehouses and airbases.

In addition to the above, I ought to mention that any reasonably complete investigation of the defeat in its entirety cannot neglect the subject of Arab underdevelopment in scientific, technical, and economic areas. For since the first Arab-Israeli war, preparation for the battle for liberation has been conceived conventionally, in terms of preparing a modern organized army for large military battles within a classical military strategy. Military preparation has yet to include any serious role for guerrilla war or concede but the narrowest scope to the popular war of liberation. Even the Palestinian Liberation Army has been established along the lines of regular armies, as it appears, including its fedayeen brigades and shock troops. In other words, when we turn our attention to studying and analyzing the defeat in order to derive lessons and warnings from it, we must begin our investigation with

---

1   See the study of Dr. Sa'd al-Deen Ibrahim, *Al-Harb al-Scha'biyyah wa'l-Ta'bi'at al-'Amah* [*Popular War and General Mobilization*], Beirut, *Dirasat 'Arabiyyah*, August 1968, and the article of Dr. Jamal Humdan, "Nahnu wa'l-Dawlat al-'A#sriyyah" ["We and the Modern State"] *Al-Fikr al-Mu'asir* (Cairo: July 1968).

how we prepared for the battle in fact (not with our subsequent conceptions of what should have been the case) and its effectiveness when put to the test in order to show the breaches, gaps, and errors that the battle exposed in our years and years of striving to prepare for it. Thus, whoever examines the defeat in this context must pay attention to the level of prevailing scientific practice, the level of available technical readiness, and the extent of our real control over our economy and its resources, in addition to the other matters that are organically and directly tied to the success of the sort of war with which the Arabs chose to confront Israel. In other words, the Arabs chose to pursue and prepare themselves for particular methods of war with Israel without sufficient awareness to the specific character of the technical, technological, scientific, and high modern achievements required of a country to undertake the mobilization for this sort of war in the second half of the twentieth century. The Arabs must not fall into the same error concerning the popular war of liberation, plunging into it without a concentrated awareness of all the factors and considerations (political, economic, organizational, ideological, logistical, etc.) that must surround, support, and accompany popular military efforts in order to achieve success and victory.

1) We need to be completely clear that the technical and scientific proficiency in a country is not defined merely by the availability of military and non-military experts, machines, and equipment, or by the availability of some industries and development projects. All of these exist in some regions of the Arab nation, and when they do not, we can import or purchase them. Their existence, in itself, does not entail that some Arab country has improved its scientific, technological, and industrial level in a tangible and effective manner that can be relied on in the hour of need and in an urgent crisis. Obtaining 200 MIG aircraft is no more than a necessity when we discover that the enemy has obtained 200 Mirage aircraft. However, such a reaction is feeble, not forming a sufficient and decisive response to the resources made available to the enemy upon its asking for this number of fighter planes. It is, rather, only the first and necessary step to make such a response. The required response entails not only equipment, machines, experts, and

aircraft, but also a particular kind of mentality, psychology, cultural background, and physical reactions that the industrial revolution implanted in modern man and the scientific revolution confirmed in him so that they became part of his nature, spontaneity, reactions, and automatic thinking , whether he is crouching in a MIG fighter plane or standing in a factory manufacturing the lubricants that enable armored vehicles to move.

In order to move beyond the level of generalities, we can cite some simple examples that show what we mean when we speak of the physical reactions that are required for skillful interaction with machines and, especially, with sophisticated, precise machines, in order to derive their fullest power and potentiality from them, and we can compare that with the specific character of the physical reactions that someone becomes accustomed to in a society in which machines do not play an important role. Primitive agricultural tools (the traditional plow, for example) form, in reality, nothing more than an extension of human limbs, and submit entirely to the rhythm of natural bodily motion and its spontaneous reactions. As for the sophisticated machine, it imposes its private rhythm on the human body and demands the training of the bodily reactions until there is harmony with the pattern of its movement. If someone fails to attain this, he is exposed to injury since any sloppiness in his movement, no matter how slight, might lead to a loss of one of his fingers or limbs, just as any carelessness, no matter how fleeting, or any deviation from the pattern of movement the machine imposes, no matter how trivial, might expose him to danger or bodily damage. The process of conforming to the rhythm of a machine is not a simple matter at all, but requires specific gifts, depending on the situation and circumstances, and often long, exhausting train- ing, absorbing years in the case of individuals and generations in the case of societies and peoples. As the machine becomes more sophisticated, the need for long training and sophisticated study increases, etc. Experts estimate that the time elapsing between a driver of a typical automobile recognizing danger emerging in front of him and the immediate reaction to avoid danger fluctuates between one-fifth and one-tenth of a second. This power of quick reaction is a skill gained, in general, as a result of practice and exer- cise. As for the pilot who flies jet planes, he must, much of the time, reduce this time segment between the recognition of danger and appropriate avoidance behavior to the limit of one-hundredth of a second, for example. This assumes a level of mental and bodily skill whose achievement is only feasible for a distinct elect of individuals, distinct in relation to their natural gifts and their practical and technical training.

We now can imagine the problems that a concerned individual will encounter in attaining these types of refined skills if he grew up in a rural society, for example, in which only primitive tools are available, and where he lacked the opportunity of interaction with sophisticated machines except relatively later in his life, whether this occurs when he flees to the city, enlists in the armed forces, or enters one of the universities in one of its science departments. Here lies the importance of the statements of the war minister in the United Arab Republic cited earlier about the illiterate soldier and the educational and scientific prerequisites for a suitable fighter, as he called him.

This conflict between sophisticated machines and the man who was formed mentally and physically in an environment not dominated by the machine is the source of the persistent doubt and continual grumbling that we always hear in societies entering the process of industrialization concerning the plague of damage due to negligence in factories and the unintentional destruction of equipment and machines, and so on. The solution to the problem does not merely depend on making the worker or responsible party understand that the machines in the factory are expensive and have the greatest importance in relation to the economy of the country and its security, and thus that it is necessary to ensure their safety and protect them from abuse. It depends, rather, primarily on new mental and physical habits that must become second nature in the person, that is, implanted in him until they become part of his spontaneity and automatic movement so that he is able to perform them without confusion or sloppiness even in hours of need, crises, and danger.

2) It emerged after the last war that the Arab armies were not lacking in military weapons and equipment, but were superior to

the Israeli army in many aspects of being armed and equipped.[1] However, what they lacked was the human element, capable and trained at a high level – technically, militarily, and in leadership. It is not possible to separate a sufficient supply of the required human element in regards to ability and preparation from the environment in which the individual grows up, the institutions that form his personality, and the social influences that give his behavior its character and rhythm. Whenever programs of modern science influence the shaping of the individual, instilling in him its mentalities and theories so that he is capable of transforming himself in compliance with its progress, then the mustering of the required human element is easier, fuller, and faster.

Thus the extent of the short-sightedness that afflicted the Arabs as they prepared their troops during the past twenty years to confront Israel in accordance with a particular type of warfare becomes evident. For they did not pay sufficient attention to the specific character of the advanced technical and scientific expertise countries require to bear the burden of this type of warfare in the second half of the twentieth century. These considerations apply especially to the process of producing sufficient quantities of the human element capable of and effective in steering the matters of a regular war to a successful conclusion. President Abdel Nasser pointed to the importance of this human element in one of his speeches:

> The Soviet Union supported us in this matter to the fullest extent possible. However, it was not a question of weapons. The human element is the decisive element for achieving victory.[2]

The Arabs are not capable of producing this decisive human element yet for many reasons, one of the most important being that the interaction between Arab society and modern industrial cultural values has been limited in most cases to taking advantage of the productive practical applications of scientific research and

---

1 See the lecture of the Chief of Staff Hasan Mustafa, *Al-Thaqafat al-'Arabiyyah* [*Arab Culture*] (Beirut: December 1967), 366.
2 *Al-Anwar*, April 30, 1968.

theory and profiting from the fruits of modern science (and industry, invention, and the technical process).

Arab society has yet to penetrate to its roots, achieve a serious understanding of its generative powers, effectively share in pushing it forward across a wide region, or even radically comply with what it imposes in the way of new thoughts and values on the society and individual. It is not far from the truth to say that the most that occurred in the Arab nation in relation to this problem is that we have opened a space in our life for the refrigerator, television, oil well, MIG, radar, and so on. However, the mentality that uses these imported achievements is still a traditional mentality that belongs to the nomadic and agrarian stages and which clings to the supernatural, that is, the stages preceding the industrial and scientific revolutions in human history. This is a strange phenomenon and one deserving concern because some non-Arab underdeveloped nations took another route during a short time. They did not content themselves with establishing contact with the values of modern culture, but instead passed with great haste beyond the stage of benefiting from the fruits of science, importing its practical applications, and exploiting them in a shallow way. Instead, they entered an industrial, scientific, and technological renaissance that radically changed the fabric of their traditional societies and exploded their pastoral values, tribal relationships, supernatural beliefs, customs depending on primitive agriculture, and cities living off risk mercantilism to make themselves important military and economic powers in international society.

In other words, the Israeli enemy was not only supplied with the most modern military weapons and destructive equipment, and with all the effective assistance that the capitalist world placed in its service, but it was also provided with a particular spirit and mentality that is entirely at home with the modern technical process, understands it completely, and knows how to take advantage of it, exploit it entirely, and glean all its possibilities. We are not able to say the same about our attitude towards the modern weapons we also possess, whose latent power and effectiveness are comparable to those of the enemy. For the rhythm of life in Arab society has failed to change enough in order to harmonize with the regular rhythm of the machine that does not get bored or grow tired! Our concepts of time and space, measurement of distance and precision in work, and skill in using sophisticated machines has failed to fall into synchronization with the technical civilization of the twentieth century and its scientific and secular culture. For example, one of the leaders of religious thought in Lebanon wrote in one of the newspapers to reassure the Arabs on the fate of military battle with Israel since, in his words, the angels that descended in the Battle of the Trench to fight on the side of the Prophet Mohammed and his allies will descend to fight on our side today and ensure for us the victory in our battle with the enemy. While the reader may smile, the truth is that the mentality that prevails with the Arab generally and in his reactions and reflections is much closer to what this learned man of religion expresses than it is to the mentality and psychology that is fully aware of how to derive the widest and furthest benefit from sophisticated machines or from the opportunities granted by the popular war of liberation. We have learned that our skills in using the plane, the tank, and the rocket is what will decide the results of the battle, but for some reason, we find ourselves compelled to utter words like those of this learned man of religion and make a partner of the angels, despite everything, in the battle. After the first round of war ceased and we recognized the defeat that the Arab nation suffered, the King of Morocco undertook to rationalize and explain it, saying that we turned away from God and God turned away from us – and thus the setback.

Ten months after the defeat, the Virgin Mary became a party to the operation of liquidating the traces of the aggression, appearing in one of the churches in Cairo, where "one of the photography studios in the suburb of Zaitun was able to photograph her during her evening appearance...Then Abba Samu'il showed the photograph to newspaper reporters in front of the television cameras."[1] The Virgin had made this appearance "to support the Egyptian people, who are faithful and blessed according to the text of the Holy Bible, in the misfortune or crisis that they are passing through now...and as a heavenly sign that God is with us and did not abandon us...and that He will come to our aid so that all will feel this crisis as only an accident and that the heavens are still on our side."[2]

---

1 *Al-Ahram*, May 5, 1968.
2 Ibid.

This appearance indicates that "the Virgin Mary is not pleased with what the Jews violated and are violating in the Holy Lands in the city of Jerusalem. What took place there grieves her as she is the protector of the Holy Lands, and thus she has come to announce to mankind her anger and grief and call for the purifying of Jerusalem of its defilers."[1]

3) One of the most urgent matters concerning the conditions of the Arab nation, especially in regards to the areas of underdevelopment we have noted, is the absence of productive scientific institutions and flourishing technical specialist institutes, and the weakness of our national universities in effectively participating in scientific research and applying it in strategic and non-strategic areas. The first institution that the Jews created in Palestine was Hebrew University. After the founding of Israel, the Weizmann Institute for scientific research flourished with a distinguished elect of scientists in nuclear and atomic physics, chemistry, mathematics, and so on. There was also a proliferation of the other technical, professional, and industrial institutes. What do we find in our Arab nation to compare with these achievements of the Israeli enemy? From the ocean to the gulf, there is only one Arab state that has undertaken an organized plan to invest in scientific research, the United Arab Republic. With its oil and its hundred million citizens, the Arab nation does not contain one institute that grants a baccalaureate or *licence* diploma in electronics, although it knows that the MIG fighter plane is replete with electronic equipment and that all radar networks depend on such equipment. Similarly, the ability to use this sophisticated equipment is not limited to guiding it in normal times and favorable circumstances, but includes also the expertise to use it in times of urgency and to interpret it correctly despite the distortion that the enemy equipment directs towards it. The source of this expertise is the "mechanical intelligence" that technical institutes are supposed to teach to technicians and specialists so that they confront these unexpected circumstances and derive the

---

1   Ibid. See my separate study of the case of the miracle published under the title "Mu'ajizat Thuhur al-'Athra' wa Tasfiyat Athar al-'Adwan" ["The Miracle of the Appearance of the Virgin and the Elimination of the Traces of Aggression"] in *Dirasat 'Arabiyyah* [*Arab Studies*] (July 1968).

greatest benefits possible from the equipment despite the obstacles they face. This sort of intelligence, and what it relies on in the way of technical expertise, cannot be gained in depth during training tours on how to use sophisticated equipment unless the interested individual possesses the basic scientific education and primary technical training that universities and technical institutes are supposed to offer their students.

In his study on modern Arab scientific thought, Dr. Wasfi Hijab demonstrated that upon reviewing one of the international journals of scientific abstracts (Science Citation Index), which publishes short summaries of every scientific study in specialty journals from all parts of the world, he found only one Arabic-language journal out of the original 1500 scientific journals cited in that journal of abstracts: *The Journal of the United Arab Republic for Chemistry*.[1] In the same study, he showed that Arab scientists published almost one thousand studies in international scientific journals in the year 1965, nine-tenths of the publications being from the United Arab Republic and the greater part of the remaining tenth being published by scientists at the American University of Beirut. As for the rest of the vast Arab nation, in regards to scientific production it is a barren and sterile desert in every meaning of the word. Dr. Hijab comments on these facts, saying, "If we take into consideration that the inhabitants of the Arab world are almost three percent of the world population and that scientific production in 1965 was almost one million scientific papers, then the Arab world contributed only three percent of its share relative to its population."

Today, no doubt, the Arab nation and its leaders are being called on to immediately establish an Arab institute for strategic studies, an Arab institute for electronics, an institute for the natural sciences, an institute for petrochemical studies, and for a fast and full reconsideration of the programs for the natural sciences, the curriculum for mathematics, and the organizations entrusted with implementing them.

---

1   In *Al-Fikr al-'Arabiyi fi Mi'at Sannah* [*Arabic Thought in One Hundred Years*], Publications of the Centenary (American University of Beirut: 1968), 604–28.

These institutes are supposed to reassemble the great number of young Arab scientists working today in different universities and scientific institutes outside the Arab homeland, in Europe and the United States specifically. However, the Arab nation is incapable of establishing and funding a number of very well-equipped scientific institutes, drawing back the scientists who scattered abroad or did not return at the end of their studies, because of the miserable conditions that prevail in our national universities in regards to science, organization, and administration.

Everyone who wrestles with these conditions knows that they do not aid the young scientist in research or production and do not provide the desired atmosphere for him to continue in productive scientific work. To the contrary, they attempt to suck up his intellectual initiative and scientific aspirations in the name of the routine and a system of regulations that goes back to past, outmoded eras, untouched by the hand of reform and change that would render it suitable to the requirements of scientific research in the second half of the twentieth century.

Moreover, often those who hold positions of responsibility in the science departments in our national universities are professors who owe their places in the university to their age, length of service, or scientific accomplishments that they performed many long years ago, left behind long ago by the advancing procession of science. Thus they have become unable to follow the new developments that occur every hour in their specialized fields. All of us know that our national universities are really institutions for testing the students at the end of the school year, not institutions for preserving, transmitting, renewing, developing, and extending human knowledge, or placing it in the service of the nation and people.

If Israel is able to gather Jewish (and non-Jewish) scientists in their scientific institutes that directly participate in all aspects of its life, why is the Arab nation unable to gather the diaspora of Arab scientists in similar institutes, enabling them to serve science, the nation, the people and its continuous renaissance, and the training of a new generation of qualified Arab scientists? There are many other examples:

1) Only one month after the establishment of the People's Republic of China, the government undertook the establishing of the Chinese Academy of Science and directed an invitation to Chinese scientists working in foreign universities to join its universities and institutes. A great many of them accepted the invitation and returned to their nation to form the nucleus around which China continues to build its modern scientific revival, the source of its growing domestic and international power. One of its most prominent achievements was in nuclear research, which it completed in a short period of time, and with only negligible foreign assistance. The Chinese scientists were able to explode their hydrogen bomb before France did, although France is considered one of the world's leading industrial states and has a long and deep scientific tradition.

2) In 1931, Stalin spoke about the quality of the giant effort that the Soviet government was exerting to overcome the economic, scientific, military, and political underdevelopment that Russia was mired in, addressing his country's scientists in the following words: "Because of its underdevelopment, the history of Russia is the history of continuous defeat...We have at most ten years to catch up with the advanced capitalist countries...Therefore, you ought to study everything and let nothing escape your attention, and to increase in knowledge day by day...We must study technology and gain complete mastery over science, etc." In spite of the destruction that the Nazi invasion left behind, the science policy of the Soviet Union took a very short time to come to complete fruition. In 1958, the American magazine *Time* mentioned in the course of criticizing some aspects of scientific life in the United States that Soviet universities and institutes were graduating twice as many engineers as American universities and institutes per year, and that the Soviet government was bestowing money almost without counting on developing both theoretical and applied scientific research, for it considered it a necessary condition for its increasing economic growth, military and political power, and international status.[1] We must recognize the importance of these facts and the significance of the experiences of other countries in relation to our present and future vis-à-vis Israel and the culture of this century.

---

1   *Time Magazine,* November 18, 1957, 7.

3) We all remember the near panic that swept the United States in the winter of 1958 after the Soviet Union succeeded in placing the first satellite into space. Scientific circles that winter were alarmed and regarded the Soviet triumph, on the one hand, and the failure of the first American attempt to place a similar satellite into space, on the other hand, as an important setback to America, with international and military significance. However, what concerns us here is the American reaction to this setback and how the Americans overcame it and eliminated its results. The first thing the expert class in America did was to take a second look at their educational programs at all levels (from primary schools to the largest nuclear laboratories) to identify their weaknesses and then strengthen or replace them to conform with the current demands of the technological, scientific, and military challenges that the country was beginning to face. As an example, I cite here the criticism that one of the senior experts in education directed to programs of secondary education in America in front of a large gathering of American scientists meeting for that purpose: "the programs for mathematics taught in our secondary institutions are anachronistic since the concepts of mathematics and physics that prevail are those that prevailed in the nineteenth century, just as they are no longer able to tie together the information taught with the science of mathematics as an integrated unit."[1] The famous nuclear scientist Edward Teller (the maker of the world's first hydrogen bomb) warned the Americans of the consequences of not taking the role of scientific research seriously in overcoming the setback, saying that "the Russians regard science as if it were a religion, and they regard their scientists with the utmost degree of respect." He then added that scientists and teachers in the United States continue to be relatively underpaid and do not enjoy a status in American society proportional to the importance of their responsibilities and the work that they do. He also emphasized that the incentives for young men and women to enter and devote themselves to purely scientific fields are currently insufficient.[2] After self-criticism and precise scrutiny, the responsible parties in the United States reached the

---

1 Ibid. November 11, 1957, 50.
2 Ibid. October 16, 1957, 16.

conclusion that overcoming the setback required two fundamental steps: 1) strengthening the country's scientific, theoretical, and applied research and pushing it ahead with urgency, especially in the vital areas in which America lags the Soviet Union; 2) reforming the scientific programs in the secondary schools and strengthening and renewing them in accordance with the national goals for growth at every level of national life.[1] In order to achieve the second step, experts undertook numerous studies about secondary institutions, the most famous study being that of Dr. James B. Conant, a famous senior scholar and the previous president of Harvard University. In it, he evaluated the secondary schools in America, exposing the weak areas and making a number of fundamental suggestions on how to raise their scientific and cultural level so that they could fulfill their obligations to support the United States across the full spectrum of its current challenges. The lesson to be drawn here for the Arabs is the necessity of responding in a way suited to treating the true source of the disease. The challenge that the Arab nation faces today is the defeat inflicted by an enemy made strong by the power of modern science, its achievements, its inventions, its technical mentality, and a psychology that is at home with machines. The Arab nation ought to begin immediately to develop effective organizations and institutions so that we can travel the road ahead of us towards a higher level of scientific preparation in order to confront our enemies effectively in the near and distant future.

4) Of course, the process of revising educational programs and reconsidering our scientific situation so that we are able to prepare competent scientists is not a simple matter that can be completed in a brief time. Thus, I suggested above that we make immediate use of Arab scientists working abroad. I want to turn to another relatively speedy option that a number of countries have adopted in order to hasten the preparation of the necessary scientists, specialists, and technicians, an experiment of which the Soviets were one of the pioneers. One of the venerable Russian traditions, and one that continues to this day, is the dedicating of special institutions

---

1   Ibid. November 18, 1957, 19.

to children possessing extraordinary artistic gifts in, for example, music or dancing (ballet) or some other fine art, in order to support them with private patronage in special curricula whose adoption is not possible for typical schools. The government of the Soviet Union applied this tradition to male and female students with exceptional gifts in mathematics, physics, and the natural sciences, teaching such curricula in secondary schools in order to produce the greatest possible number of outstanding scientists in the shortest possible time, and without wasting the time of these young geniuses in the usual school drudgery. The special curricula in mathematics include, for example, topics that are not typically taught except at the university level, like analytic geometry, theoretical mechanics, applications of mathematics to physics, differential calculus, etc. Therefore, the universities have oversight in the composition and application of these special curricula.

In 1958, President Khrushchev suggested to the central committee of the Communist Party the transforming of these special programs for geniuses to completely independent schools, saying in his report on this subject, "it is necessary to establish special schools for talented students in physics, mathematics, industrial design, and the biological sciences, etc...with the goal of preparing them to pursue their higher studies according to their special gifts."[1] James Conant, in his book cited earlier, had suggested the establishing of similar curricula in American secondary institutions.[2]

Focusing the effort on preparing a number of competent Arab scientists with these accelerated, proven methods undoubtedly deserves the attention and concern of the Arab leaders. The Soviet Union has had so much success with its programs that in 1958 Mr. Lewis Strauss, the president of the Atomic Energy Commission in the United States, admonished the Americans: "I can learn of no public high school in our country where a student obtains so thorough a preparation in science and mathematics, even if he seeks it – even if he should be a potential Einstein."[3]

---

1   N. Dewitt, *Education and Professional Employment in the USSR,* 18, 19.
2   James B. Conant, *The American High School,* 58, 62.
3   *Time,* November 18, 1957, 20.

If the Arabs were to compare themselves with Israel, then the words of Strauss would apply to our schools and our scientific situation entirely.

The gist of the account is that the forces of revolution in the Arab nation, and especially in the more progressive Arab countries, must now more than ever strive to introduce the Arab nation into the realm of the twentieth century, in its science, planning, industry, economy, and technical process, by adopting firmly and decisively modern science and technology, and giving both priority and precedence in economic, social, and cultural planning. It must also support the course of fundamental change that traditional Arab society must undergo to accord with the demands of the industrial and scientific revolution and to march according to the demands of the social, socialist, and cultural revolution we seek.

VI

In a speech that President Abdel Nasser gave to the workers in the United Arab Republic, he said:

> Whenever we speak about the Arab patriotism or Arab nationalism, we must at this stage forget many other concepts. The left-wing nationalist is the same as the right-wing nationalist, because Israel, when it occupied the West Bank of the Jordan, did not distinguish between the left-wing nationalist and right-wing nationalist as long as both of them were nationalists.[1]

These words appear to acknowledge the impotence that struck the socialist Arab revolutionary movement as exemplified in the ruling regimes, and their forces, orientations, and policies. I do not mean this in the manner of the right-wing reactionary criticism that

---

1   *Al-Ahram,* April 16, 1968.

exploits the defeat as an excuse to reject the socialist revolution altogether, this radical revolution that Arab society must attain if it wants staying power, continuity, and progress in this era. The Arab revolutionary movement had many successes in the areas of economic emancipation (in some of the Arab countries), freedom from traditional political dependence, the battle against colonialism, etc. However, the June defeat showed that the socialist Arab revolution is not sufficiently revolutionary and not sufficiently socialist when measured by the strict standards that the defeat imposes rather than by relative standards, that is, by comparison to the Arab condition before the rise of the revolution. If we have mischaracterized the situation, then what forced President Abdel Nasser to nullify the distinctions between the right and the left in the speech he gave in front of a group of Arab workers and dilute the sharp differences between the two orientations? For the source of these differences is the social and scientific socialist content of the idea of Arab nationalism, and the primary credit for giving the idea of Arab nationalism its social and socialist dimensions on the plane of practical successes goes to the Arab progressive movement led by Nasser himself. The fifteen-year-old Arab revolution is supposed to find its support and center – in the hours of trial and crises – in its revolutionary social content and its socialist merits alone, not in a return of the concept of Arab nationalism in which the right-wing reactionary and left-wing scientific socialist standpoint are considered equals. This equivalence is, in fact, entirely unacceptable because the elimination of the distinction between the left and the right in regards to Arab nationalism is entirely to the advantage of the right. It cannot be considered a type of passing tolerance, granting the right and the forces of reaction a role because of current circumstances.

The Arab right today exists in abundance and without fear: it is at ease and shares in the affluence enjoyed by Arab reactionaries and their neo-colonialist supporters. In contrast to this favorable situation for the Arab right, the nullification that President Abdel Nasser referred to demonstrates that a true Arab socialist left capable of leading the Arab nation during its current trial does not exist, despite everything that was said to indicate the opposite, whether before or after the defeat.

The words of President Abdel Nasser do not mean that the Arab socialist revolutionary movement will tolerate the Arab right during this stage for the sake of mobilizing all powers under its leadership and banner, but that the demand from the right is that it will tolerate the revolutionary movement in the current crisis and not add to its misery and unhappiness. All of this is clear from the Saudi and Kuwaiti attitude, for example, towards the idea of establishing a united military leadership for the armies of the Arab states adjacent to the occupied territory. The newspaper *Al-Hayat* summed up this attitude as follows:

> Informed sources close to the Saudi and Kuwaiti delegations say that the two rulers will not resist the establishing of this leadership on the condition that there is a change in the political direction of some Arab states, including their emancipation from imported principles.[1]

In other words, the change in direction means that these states renounce their socialist and revolutionary character. The same newspaper cited a report confirming the same fact and direction:

> King Faysal and Emir Sabah feel that the policy that led to the last disaster is still in place and taking the same path as it was before the 5th of June, and they are concerned that the continuation of this policy will increase Soviet meddling and penetration in addition to paving the way for the increase of the presence and influence of the Soviets in the region.[2]

Another example: Upon Libya's paying the third installment of its financial commitment to the United Arab Republic and Jordan, the semi-official Libyan newspaper *Al-Haqiqa* raised the subject of the assistance that the Arab summit conference decided on after the war and mentioned that there were better uses for this money:

---

1   *Al-Hayat,* April 9, 1968.
2   *Al-Hayat,* April 11, 1968.

What Libya paid was not out of its surplus, but a piece of a loaf of bread and a part of the money that is allocated to the opening of a street or the building of a hospital or school.

Then the newspaper emphasized that "Libya must have a say in the spending of its money."[1]

Since we are upon the course of self-criticism, I will mention some of the active negative aspects in the structure of what we agree on calling the Arab socialist revolutionary line because they are greatly responsible for its weakness and the fragmentation that emerged when it was put to the test and subjected to harsh, severe, pitiless trials.

1) There was much discussion in the ranks of the Arab left before and after the war about the rising of an "Arab Vietnam" and about the affinity of the Arab revolution to the major socialist revolutions (the Soviet Union and China) and their stances towards America and the new colonialism. In this matter, we must be frank with ourselves that the claim of a resemblance and similitude between the present Arab revolution and the major socialist revolutions and Vietnam does much wrong and injustice to these latter revolutions and their enormous achievements. Some may consider this judgment harsh, but who of us today does not prefer treating oneself harshly rather than carelessly and with indulgence. While someone was remarking about the Arab revolution butting heads with the imperialist Americans, comparisons and claims of resemblance between the situations of the Soviet Union and China and that of the Arab revolution towards America and the new imperialism arose. The remarks concluded with the tumblers wrestling with the steers as a tactic to befuddle the American head.[2] Disregarding the advantages of this suggested tactic, and its depravities, it appears to me that the comparison between the nature and elements of the Arab revolutionary forces and the stances of the major socialist states, including with them Vietnam, gives us too much credit. For we have never been in greater need of advice from those who

---

1   *Al-Nahar*, May 19, 1968.
2   See the article by Heikal in *Al-Ahram,* August 4, 1967.

preceded us on the road of socialist struggle, whether concerning the internal or external front, learning from their experience on how to resolutely follow the socialist line in difficult days, and taking full advantage of their proven scientific and practical experience, along with their legacy of struggle, thought, and science. We need to recognize these facts lest we deceive ourselves and distort them in the manner of the clever personality who claims to rely on resources, abilities, and achievements that are illusory, having no existence in reality.

2) In contrast to the other socialist revolutions, the Arab revolution has yet to proclaim, in a frank, clear, and official way, the scientific character of its socialism and its secularism. This reluctance continues to prevail in its circles. Similarly, the Arab revolutionary forces have yet to realize the depth of the tie between socialism and modern science, and that distinguishing the socialism we seek from the other socialist ideas by its appellation "scientific socialism" is neither vain nor futile, but rather that one of its goals is to indicate that they are inseparable. Moreover, the Arab revolution is still reluctant about a number of essential matters in contrast to the socialist revolutions we compare ourselves with: Does the Arab revolution want merely to accomplish an agricultural reform that breaks up property by distributing it to individuals or does it want an agricultural revolution that industrializes agriculture and organizes the land according to the nature of production and on the basis of carefully considered scientific principles? Does the Arab revolution want to achieve real estate reform or does it want to destroy the idea of private property in the production of wealth and in everything that leads to exploitation? Does the Arab revolution want merely to transfer the means of production and the sources of wealth in the country to the public sector or does it want, in addition, to accomplish a revolution in the means and methods of production and distribution, and in the social and class relations connected with it and expressive of it? Does the Arab revolution want that human life in Arab society remains subject to a combination of religious legal prescriptions that descended to us fourteen centuries ago and laws that we inherited from the French Napoleonic Code (and the bourgeois judgments that conform with it), or does the

revolution want to revolt against the prevailing practices in order to exchange it for a contemporary legal system derived from scientific socialist thought and its elements? Does the Arab revolution want merely to reform our educational systems (at all levels), which are composed from a bizarre mix of antique traditional pedagogic ideas and styles and what we imported from the educational curricula of the French Third Republic, for example, or does it want a radical revolution against them that would direct it along the road of unrelenting progress in order to become worthy of a socialist revolution that lives in the second half of the twentieth century? The Arab revolution, as we have learned from its different stages, has yet to answer these questions with clarity, especially at the level of effective implementation, and it has only undertaken a fraction of the effective steps and clear practical measures for settling these questions to the advantage of revolutionary solutions. We cannot say the same thing about the other socialist revolutions we compare ourselves with since they have given a revolutionary answer from the beginning and taken secure practical steps to translate them into social and economic fact in the course of less than five years from the day of their birth. The defeat prescribes for the Arab revolution the abandoning of the vortex of "middle-roadism" in thought, planning, and implementation in order finally to escape the dominance of the imperialists.

Let us mention here that colonialism has never been able to root out any socialist revolution that was firmly established and clear in its thinking and practice, although it made efforts to crush the October Revolution and assailed the Chinese Revolution (planting a quasi-Israel in Formosa) and the revolutions in Korea, Cuba, and Vietnam, all in vain. As for the liberation movements among what was called before the 5th of June the Third World, they failed in their revolutionary journey towards socialism, not surpassing the stage of "non-alignment" and "positive neutrality," and thus fell as a tasty morsel to the new imperialist powers. India clearly committed itself to the capitalist camp, and after the fall of Sukarno and Nkrumah and others, here was the Israeli army of occupation perched on our Arab lands. In other words, the societies of Arab countries that were overseen by forces that considered themselves revolutionary and leftist were still, in essence, built on the old basis that we wish to see exploded in whole and part for the sake of a socialist, industrial, and scientific transformation. In spite of everything the Arabs have said about the revolutionary spirit, this basis remains in existence, whether in regard to legislation, the system of education, the individual organization of agriculture, the administrative bureaucracy, the personal statutes, or the tribal loyalties and clan ties that still determine a great part of the human relationships and the like of the people and institutions in Arab society. All of this persists in the shade of the progressive regimes themselves, and under their ears and eyes.

One of the consequences of this deficiency in ideological clarity that prevails in the Arab socialist movement and inclines it towards middle-roadism is the sterile argument concerning whether the socialism that the Arab revolutionary forces should advocate is "Arab socialism" or "an Arab application of socialism," and whether our socialism is scientific, dogmatic, imported, rational, judicious, or Islamic, or something else belonging to this style of intellectual chatter and verbal sophistry whose effects are reflected in both theory and practice. This sterile argument has no connection to any serious and significant attempt to determine the identity of the Arab left. Its essence, in fact, does not go beyond risible attempts to anoint itself with the word socialism because of the positive meanings and fine echoes that the word enjoys with the Arab masses in order to camouflage standpoints, measures, and policies that have no connection to scientific socialism. The articles that are written about the verbal distinctions in play in the differences between "Arab socialism" and "an Arab application of socialism" are, indeed, nothing more than tricks with which we divert ourselves from the chief matter that ought to be the target of our intellectual and scientific concerns, scientific socialism in itself. Unless we say that they are tricks that aim to falsify the situation and distort the serious attempts to understand it and the role of the Arab left in regards to it. The Lebanese writer Dr. Hasan Sa'ab spreads a layer of philosophical, historical, and cultural legitimacy around the standpoint of middle-roadism that applied (and still applies) to the Arab liberation movements in general and the advanced regimes in particular, saying:

These progressive examples, models, and experiences (outside the Arab world) possess something that is agreeable and something that is disagreeable. We are now used to saying that we want Islam to mediate between the two, because God made us an intermediary nation, "Let us be witnesses to the people." Because the Prophet taught us the better part of the thing is the middle, and because our geographical position is in the middle, and because our cultural experience is an experience of being in the middle, between the East and West, or between Eastern Asia and Western Europe, or between the Western rationality of the Greeks and the pantheism of Eastern Asia. The time has approached that we confirm that creative mediation is not imitative or fabricated mediation, if we want to protect our freedom, genius, authenticity, and novelty.[1]

The one conclusion that might be drawn from Dr. Sa'ab's justification of middle-roadism is that we are, in the final analysis, a people lacking both stance and authenticity, and that we have nothing to offer except to mediate between the authenticities of others, for which we share no credit, and between the deep-seated stances assumed by other peoples, nations, and civilizations. Moreover, from a practical standpoint, Dr. Sa'ab's argument entails the defense of the Arab status quo and its social, economic, and political privileges, the defense of its security and the call for matters to run according to "their natural courses," deferring to the middle of the road in which we stand and rationalizing it, whatever the results. In the end, a moderate reforming platform in the name of religion and tradition, and progress also, entirely rejects a direct radical intervention with the goal of changing, shaking, and overturning the status quo, as the revolutionary scientific socialist logic advocates for it in ways that we believe are crucial if the Arabs are to confront the challenges that agitate them today at all levels of their existence. This middle-roadism was even reflected in the circles that are supposed to represent the Arab scientific socialist left in the United Arab Republic, and there are some who spread, rationalize,

---

1   "Al-islam wa tahadiyyat al-hayati al-'asriyah" ["Islam and the Challenges of Contemporary Life"] (Hiwar: July–August, 1965), 31.

and give it a philosophical veneer to the point where a group there has emerged from this left with a novel, strange, odd composition, its name being the socialist-scientific-Islamic-fideistic party.[1]

One of the results of the obscurity that surrounds the ideas of the Arab revolution and the consequences of its practical successes is the flood of superficial conceptions of what it means to establish the socialist state according to the idea of the Arab revolutionary movement. I mean by this conceptions that do not exceed the stage of agricultural reform and nationalization (industrial reform) and merely create an atmosphere of approval among the toiling classes by transferring to some of its members a piece of land or distributing some monetary sums to them from the profits of the factories that they have become owners of by virtue of their having become now part of the public sector. These regulations and their analogues spring from a mentality that still rotates in the orbit of a fluid, unstable concept of private property, one that has yet to comprehend the scientific socialist concept of property. The same thing can be said in relation to the kind of superficial interest the progressive Arab regimes show in heritage, tradition, religious values, popular theater, popular literature, and popular art, etc. For because of the intellectual and practical middle-roadism from which the Arab revolution suffers, this concern has turned into a concealed reactionary resistance to the scientific progress, scientific socialist practice, and the cultural revolution that societies walking these paths seek. All this in the name of defending the people's traditions, values, art, and heritage, when it actually shields popular supernaturalisms, superstitions, ignorance, and backward worn-out values, regurgitating the old in its obsolescence and leaving social conditions and human relations as they are, that is, in a condition of severe backwardness.

There is, no doubt, no life in the Arab revolutionary movement except in its reliance, to the greatest extent, on the popular will, the working masses, and the toiling classes as the rising historical force.

---

1   See, for example, the following articles in the Egyptian magazine *Al-Katib*: Dr. Mohammed Ahmed Khalif Allah, "Al-quran al-karim wa'l-madamin al-ishtirakiyah" ["The Noble Koran and Implications of Socialism"] July 1966, 'Abd al-Mufti Sa'id, "Al-tajribat al-ishtirakiyyat al-'arabiyyah" ["The Arab Socialist Experiments"] January 1967 and March 1967.

However, this does not mean that the situation of the Arab masses in terms of mentality, personality, education, culture, and society, etc. does not need a radical, fundamental, and revolutionary correction. Obviously, the Arab masses are sinking under a heavy burden of feelings, sensations, methods of expression, and styles of thinking that are the product of hundreds of years of cultural decline and deep intellectual and scientific stagnation. This burden is ready to resist progress, revolution, socialism, and every substitute and change in Arab life, by merely the force of its latent inertia. Because of this heritage of underdevelopment and inferiority, we find the great majority of the Arab masses believe much more in magic and myth than they believe in tangible facts, prefer the medical advice of a sheikh or sorcerer to a consultation with a medical specialist, and are stirred much more by religious mumbling than the most important scientific discovery or the most significant industrial invention in the world. The point of the existence of the progressive and socialist system in the Arab nation is the revolution against this Arab burden of backwardness, not concluding a truce with it, adapting to it, adjusting to it, or refraining from aiming socialist revolutionary measures against it, with the excuse of "deferring to the feelings of the religious masses" in the name of "the shock that those who still cling to antique traditions and ancient superstitions will suffer" or in the name of defending traditions and preserving the people's heritages, along with the rest of these excuses and apologies. When middle-roadist progressive regimes conclude a truce with inclinations towards backwardness and deteriorating cultural inferiority and adjust to them, suitably or unsuitably, they do this at the expense of the true interests of the toiling Arab masses since this sort of behavior condones ignorance, backwardness, clannishness, dependence, and the supernatural, that is, it allows the decaying cultural situation to persist despite the fact that the Arab people in the twentieth century have only reaped from it disasters, setbacks, tragedies, and weakness.

On this subject, I want to discuss an article by Elias Sahab in which he attempts to deny the adjective of middle-roadist to the Nasser regime and to claim that it was "the pioneering socialist revolutionary regime in the Third World." Furthermore, he mentions in the course of this something about building regimes in the

Third World according to "the non-capitalist road" and argues the following:

> The regime of Abdel Nasser is the regime of national social-
> ist revolution within the Third World scope of circumstances.
> Nasser did not choose these circumstances at will, but rather
> it [the regime] was a natural result of his assuming power
> in a particular patch of the world in a particular historical
> circumstance.[1]

When we reproach Nasser's regime with its middle-roadism in theory and practice, we are never overlooking the circumstances that the Third World submitted to and that President Abdel Nasser was forced to work within. Thus, I believe that the policy of non-alignment and positive neutrality and the slogan of a non-capitalist course of national development has served the Arab cause to the greatest extent in one of its important stages of development and achieved great positive revolutionary results to its benefit. There is no doubt that the greatest credit for these achievements is due to President Abdel Nasser's extraordinary leadership in the United Arab Republic. Likewise, attributing middle-roadism to Nasser's regime and criticizing it on this basis is not a novelty that we have introduced but a fundamental issue broached in Arab Marxist leftist circles and in Egypt itself more than any other place. Everyone who consults the Egyptian journal *Al-Tali'ah* [*The Vanguard*] and the journal *Al-Katib* [*The Writer*] will be convinced of this, especially in regards to the articles that were published immediately after the defeat.[2]

However, it appears to me that middle-roadism became an urgent problem because the Third World circumstances that Elias Sahab spoke about had radically changed and the particular historical circumstance in which President Abdel Nasser assumed power in a patch of the Third World had changed even more radically, especially after the defeat of the 5th of June. Moreover,

---

1   *Al-Muharrer,* Beirut, April 29, 1968.
2   See also the articles of the Egyptian writer Salah 'Issa in the magazine *Al-Hurriya* [*Freedom*] (September 12, 19, 26, 1966), and the articles of Mohammed Kashli in the same magazine (July 25, August 8, 15, 22, 1966).

that generated the obvious truth that the freezing of Arab politics within the limits of applying slogans that initially make their case negatively, like "a non-capitalist road," "positive neutrality," "non-alignment," and "the Third World" (which is supposed to mediate between the first and second world) will lead to crippling of revolutionary Arab politics in its confrontation with the existing Zionist challenge, no matter at what level we want this confrontation to take place, whatever the circumstances. The same can be said in relation to the similarly middle-roadist slogans and ideas proposed for domestic socialist policy like: "non-exploitive capitalism," "non-exploitive property," "the dissolution of differences between classes," and "no domination of one class over the other." At this stage, halting at the slogan "non-exploitive capitalism," for example, becomes merely the consecration of the traditional economic practice that considers work nothing more than a commodity, even if we give this consecration a legal disguise by means of the expressions "rightful and reasonable profit" and the like. It is enough that we know that the masses of peasants, workers, and toilers form the great majority of the Arab people for us to realize to what extent the slogan "no domination of one class by another" is partial to the classes that own property, have leisure, and enjoy special privileges, and to what extent it is inimical, in the end, to the interests of the brutalized proletariat and toiling masses.[1]

The matter is similar in regards to the slogan "no sacrifice of the present generation for the sake of future generations," which at the practical level comes to mean no sacrifice in the material and non-material privileges enjoyed by old and new groups and classes that float at the surface of society and enjoy a high standard of living and consumption at the expense of the popular base and of the basic requirements and goals of national development.

The effectiveness of the revolution in violent and bloody struggles against occupation, colonialism, alliances, the grand bourgeoisie, and feudalism at home did not intercede for it in the following

---

1 See the appendix at the end of this study for a number of real examples concerning the middle-roadism of the regime in the United Arab Republic at the level of theory and practice.

stages or prevent its falling victim to the blow that Israel and the new colonialism directed towards it. Let us ask some drastic questions concerning what Elias Sahab said in his article about "the pioneering socialist revolution in the Third World." Where is this Third World today? Does there really exist something by the name of the Third World following the June War and its aftermath? Certainly, the Third World exists as a "geographical expression." However, as an active power shaping world events, capable of imposing its independent presence on various international blocs, it no longer has an effective existence. In the best of appraisals and probabilities, the Third World today is only a much fainter echo of what it was at an earlier stage. Elias Sahab represents an Arab orientation that still clings to the mirage of this, no doubt, exceptional stage, and yearns for it, while what is required is total and complete supersession. For after the leading regimes of national liberation in the Third World were annihilated (and in their own house), the Third World encountered another almost annihilating blow in the Arab defeat at the hands of Israel. In the wake of this, the "pioneering Arab socialist revolution in the Third World," according to the expression of Elias Sahab, fell so low that it was unable to do more than have the official speaker of the United Arab Republic, Mohammed Hasan al-Zaiyat, appeal to the member states in the Security Council to pressure Israel to implement the decision of the Security Council concerning the withdrawal of the Israeli forces from the Arab lands occupied after the 5th of June 1967. Compare, then, this waning revolutionary condition in the Third World with that represented in the exiting of Indonesia from the United Nations, this exiting that was full of the spirit of challenge and self-confidence. The likes of this comparison will make plain to us whether the Third World exists after the 5th of June.

Finally, let us ask what is this non-capitalist road for building the country that Elias Sahab mentioned, and on what basis can it rest today? On the rubble of the Nkrumah's philosophy of "consciencism"? On the clear "ideological" legacy that was transmitted from Sukarno to Suharto? On the opinions of the great propagandist for the politics of non-alignment, Krishna Menon, who is no longer heard from in his political isolation today? Or commencing from the unconditional Arab acceptance of the Security Council resolution [*242, trans. note*], the revolution, after it has agreed to the secure borders of Israel as stated by the same Security Council resolution, will pursue a "non-capitalist course of progress," while Dayan comments frankly about the secure borders, saying: "The security of Israel is where its army stands."[1] When I look now at the relevant matters and facts around me, I do not see anything by the name of the Third World, but I see the "Second World" appearing clearly and heroically in Vietnam, in Cuba, and in the will of the other socialist peoples standing beside Vietnamese and Cuban determination actively, morally, and materially. I see, also, in contrast to that, "The First World," as it appears in Vietnam itself, ineffective in its invasion, napalm, fleets, and flying fortresses (from B-52s to F-111s), and as it appears around Cuba with its economic embargo, intelligence agencies, and its exposed, scandalous assassination attempts. In other words, unless the Arab revolutionary movement succeeds in stepping beyond this middle-roadism by adopting clear and challenging scientific socialist positions, I fear that it will meet, in the end, the fate of the Third World bloc itself and become no more than a "historical expression," as the Third World has become only a "geographical expression."

When discussing the topic of middle-roadism, we need to also review the slogan "the elimination of the traces of the aggression," lending it some scrutiny in the light of the development of events, a year after it was proposed.

Maybe we can see what remains of its significance and its benefits for the Palestinian case after the Arab policies presently in place have fallen under the sway of a climate created by the diplomatic solution and the Arab rallying around the Jarring mission. The writer and commentator Ghassan Kanafani raised the issue of this slogan by formulating the important question: "Do we want the Security Council resolution [242] to be the solution to the Palestinian question or to be a solution to the traces of the aggression only?"[2] I want to discuss this subject from another angle: Are we able to truly distinguish between the solution of the Palestinian question and the solution to the problem of eliminating the traces

---

1   *Al-Nahar,* May 28, 1968, 8.

2   *Al-Anwar,* May 19, 1968.

of the aggression? Eliminating the traces of aggression in its simplest sense means the withdrawal of the Israeli army of occupation – for whatever reason – to its bases before the 5th of June, 1967. However, it appears that any Arab military attempt to eliminate the traces of the aggression by forcing the Israeli army behind its previous borders through war and combat will be met with a bold military defense on the part of Israel to avoid this forced retreat. That is, Israel will defend the lands occupied after June as forcefully as it will defend its previous borders, with the same zeal, resolve, and violence. In other words, any attempt to eliminate the traces of the aggression by way of war (conventional or popular) will entail a complete military confrontation with Israel without any distinction or difference between its previous borders and the borders of "the traces of the aggression."

If the Arab military forces (conventional and popular) are able to resist the Israeli army, push it forcefully backwards, and compel it to withdraw from the regions of the "traces of the aggression," the victorious Arab forces will not stop at the old Israeli border using as a pretext their success in eliminating the traces of the aggression and hoping to return later for the final battle for the liberation of Palestine! Since Israel is entirely aware of this, it will make a final valiant defense of the regions it gained as "traces of the aggression" against any Arab military attack to eliminate the traces of the aggression by force because it knows that the defeat of its army in the regions occupied in the June war entails its defeat as a nation and its demise as an existing political reality. In fact, there is no difference at all between forcefully eliminating the traces of the aggression and entering the war anew with Israel. That is, the military solution for eliminating the traces of the aggression entails encroaching on Israel itself, and this means nothing different than, from a practical perspective, the military solution to eliminate Israel as a state and the solution to the issue of Palestine in the way of total war with the goal of destroying its state and winning the battle for liberation.

Clearly, the question of the elimination of the traces of the aggression, as it is officially posed today, cannot mean anything but their elimination by political settlement. This means – practically – the acceptance of the existence of Israel as a reality in the region, but without negotiating with it, signing an agreement with it, or recognizing it. Once more, it is not possible to separate the problem of eliminating the traces of the aggression from the existence of Israel and, consequently, from the issue of Palestine, since an Israeli withdrawal for political reasons will effectively mean its survival here to some unnamed time, with all that this survival entails in the conversion of the Palestinian issue, in time, to a memory. This is clear from the decision of the Security Council that the Arabs accepted officially and entirely, and without reservations or conditions, although it cites "the cessation of the state of hostility" and "respect for the sovereignty of every state in the region" and "the guarantee of secure and recognized borders for all," etc.[1] That implies a conversion of the relationship of the Arab states with Israel to a relationship resembling that of the United States towards the People's Republic of China, where there are no agreements, negotiations, or recognitions.

Let us return now to the question of Ghassan Kanafani: "Do we want the decision of the Security Council as the solution to the Palestinian question or as a solution to the traces of the aggression only?" There is nothing found with the name of a solution to "the traces of the aggression only" in isolation from the Palestinian question. This is impossible militarily and impossible politically. The military solution means a violent confrontation with Israel as a whole, and if we succeed in eliminating the traces of the aggression, we will have succeeded also in solving the Palestinian problem. The political solution (the Security Council resolution) means confirming Israel and guaranteeing its existence, and even if that resolution succeeds in eliminating the traces of the aggression, it will have succeeded also in solving the Palestinian question to the advantage of Israel.

---

1   See the statements of Mr. Mahmoud Riyad, Foreign Minister of the United Arab Republic, concerning this subject, in *Al-Anwar* (May 12, 1968). See also the important conference in which three of the Jordanian ministers participated, as published in *Al-Anwar* (August 4, 1968). It emerges from the words of the ministers, and unambiguously so, that the official Arab concern today revolves solely around exiting the present ordeal by way of a peaceful and diplomatic solution and the resolution [242] of the Security Council, and denouncing Israel for rejecting that resolution.

In summary, the slogan of eliminating the traces of the aggression alone is meaningless and hopeless. We ought to flee from it as quickly as possible since if we are really serious about the original question, the question of the liberation of Palestine, then we must confront Israel actively in a war of liberation, and then it makes no difference if Israel stands within its old borders or within the new borders in the regions associated with "the traces of the aggression."

3) We all know that the peoples and developing states that adopted scientific socialism as a way to advance and develop quickly relied to the utmost on mobilizing all of the human resources available to them in the service of their national and progressive goals and in their battle against backwardness, dependency, weakness, and colonialist attacks, whatever their form. In other words, these societies and revolutionary states succeeded in converting the increasing human resources in their countries from a traditional problem and entrenched and inherited bane named "the problem of increasing population" to one of the chief natural sources of mental, physical, and technical human power in every field of achievement and development. We cannot help but mention here that the Arab revolutionary movement as it is embodied in the progressive regimes has made scant progress in these areas and has yet to make a serious attempt to convert the Arab masses to effective organized human and mental resources to confront the present cultural challenges or the burning Zionist military challenges.

The greatest example of entirely wasted Arab human resources is the completely and utterly excluded half of the Arab people, and I mean by this Arab women. When we observe the matter from this angle, we see that the Arab people do not comprise one hundred million people, as the broadcasts tell us, but only fifty million. Arab women form today, undoubtedly, the greatest reserves of latent human power in our society, still unused and untouched. It is the greatest bloc of raw intellectual and human material that the nation possesses that does not benefit the Arab revolutionary movement in any aspect. One of the most important indications of the degree of success and progress that a socialist regime has achieved in pushing its society forward, and especially in modern industry, is how widely it has used all the available human, mental, and technical resources, and whether this mobilization has discriminated between individuals on any basis but skill, training, sincerity, talent, and intelligence. This kind of growing, dynamic society truly advancing on the road of scientific socialism does not have time to waste in a sterile argument concerning the qualifications of women to enter the factory or their remaining at home because the necessity of growth, progress, and socialist transformation is what decides the argument. The Proclamation of the 30th of March in the United Arab Republic specifies "the constitution affirms the importance of regarding labor as the sole measure of human value."[1] This is a great progressive principle that a socialist revolutionary regime should have employed from the beginning, not only after the defeat. When we assess the situation based on the principle mentioned, we find that women in their present condition in Arab society have no human value at all, even in the more advanced and progressive Arab societies. We will not benefit from this principle unless it is converted speedily to detailed legislation organizing the life of society in detail and becomes a part of daily practice to the point that half the Arab people gain their human value through their labor and production. Nor will we benefit from this important principle unless it is complemented with other socialist principles that continue to go unapplied in the progressive Arab countries, despite their being among the principles of socialist systems everywhere. In other words, the legislation, customs, and habits existing in that part of the Arab world that has adopted socialism are a long way from viewing women through the lens of "labor as the sole measure of human value." That is, on the basis of her economic, social, and cultural independence, regarding her as a working member of the society and as one of its active, productive powers. In reality, Arab socialists themselves still view women through romantic ideas of motherhood and the raising of future generations, and through tribal values that revolve around dignity, sexual honor, and obedience to the husband, and that "men are the protectors and maintainers of women," and "have been preferred [by God] over them by one notch."[2]

---

1 *Al-Anwar,* March 31, 1968.
2 We will use this occasion to remind the Arab socialist revolutionaries what Karl

Adib Ka'war tells us in his book on Jewish women in Israel that when the French author Simone de Beauvoir visited Israel in April 1967 and wanted to get to know the Jewish women who left their imprint on the creation of Israel and contributed to the colonizing of Palestine, she went to interview working women in the kibbutz and women working in cities and in free professions.[1] If Simone de Beauvoir wanted to get to know the Arab women who left their imprint on the creation of the Arab liberation movement and participated in the building of modern progressive societies in the Arab states possessing revolutionary regimes, to whom would she have turned? To the heads of the official women's unions? To the society ladies busy with the Red Cross and Red Crescent? In truth, there is nothing called the Arab working woman who left her fingerprints on the formation of modern Arab society. Zionism knew from its beginning how to benefit from all the human powers available to it without exception, but the Arab revolutionary movement has not yet managed to learn this. Adib Ka'war says in his above-mentioned book:

> During the successive Arab revolutions [in Palestine], Jewish women participated in the defense of Jewish settlements, repeating this in the revolutions of 1924 and 1936–1939, when Jewish women were conscripted and those among them carrying weapons protected the Jewish lines of communication.[2]

Similarly, he cites the text of the proclamation to Jewish women to join the foreign women's division belonging to the British army with the goal of fighting the Germans and benefiting from the opportunity to train in military work for the sake of distant goals. The proclamation said:

Marx mentioned about this subject: "We are always able to determine the extent of the development of a particular historical era by the degree of the progress of women on the road to freedom...the degree of emancipation of women represents the natural measure for the general emancipation." *Writings,* Marx/Engels, Russian edition, volume 2, 337.

1   Adib Ka'war, *Al-Mar'at al-Yehudiyyah fi Filistin al-Muhtalah* [*Jewish Women in Occupied Palestine*], PLO Research Center, Beirut, 9.

2   Ibid. 156.

Jewish women feel a duty of participation in the struggle against the enemy of our people. We know that we possess the competence to confront this test just as we know that the national duty drives us to volunteer in this urgent hour. We strive to work within Jewish combat forces operating alongside other forces drawn from many nationalities under the command of the British leadership, where room is made for Jewish women to dedicate all their abilities not only in support services but also in military work itself, just as they work beside men in the days of peace.[1]

We see the same thing today in Vietnam, which mobilizes all its available human resources without exception. A Vietnamese writer says the following:

The women's army, "the army of long hair," is feared for its perseverance and fearlessness by officers, functionaries, and workers...This direct participation of the masses, especially the women among them, has played a decisive role in the war.[2]

The following is an excerpt of what one of the Syrian-Jewish girls wrote who went to Palestine to leave her imprint on the process of its colonization, the expelling of its people, and the building of the Israeli entity:

I still remember what happened on December 19th, 1943, though almost two years have passed from this date on which we arrived in the homeland. Time has passed quickly. On the outside, we are still the same "Syrian" girls, as they call us. Just as it appears that we still possess this eastern softness, however, on the inside, many changes have occurred in how we think, our perceptions, and our hopes. I remember well how we looked down on work in our first days here. Long pants and high boots – the clothes of work – were very strange to us. However, when I returned to Syria to see my family, I could

---

1   Ibid. 157.
2   Translation by Fawaz Tarablisi, *Dirasat 'Arabiyyah* [*Arab Studies*], May, 1968, 80.

not help but notice that my friends there had not changed at all and were still concerned chiefly with things like beautiful clothes, silk stockings, jewelry, and the rest.

I will tell you something strange that happened to me during my visit. One of my friends came to visit me, adorned with gold bracelets. This appeared strange to me since I had not seen this sort of jewelry for a long time. I sneered at her and asked her if the rattle of the bracelets was more important than the land that gave many of the people their daily bread. She replied to my question with a laugh. I thought to myself: How many of our people are still far from Zionism and how much work is still ahead of us to bring them over.[1]

While the enemy looks at women in terms of work clothes – long pants and high boots – and the land that gives man his daily bread, Arab women are still prisoners of "the rattle of golden bracelets," with all the negative consequences that this expression implies, and this under the supervision of the progressive socialist Arab regimes, both their eyes and ears.

It appears to me that a great number of the revolutionary Arab youth – whether they are officially committed to a progressive socialist political organization or not – will embrace this view of women (because of their traditional dispositions and entrenched conservative education) as long as it is a kind of masculine leniency towards the "fair" or "weak" sex, or a type of indulgence, disdain, or concession towards women on the part of their male superiors, in terms of mind, body, and the rest of the well-known myths. This view is more common among the educated among them, the students, thinkers, and writers, than those from other groups. However, to understand the matter in this superficial way is inimical to true socialist revolutionary ideas and practices. Thus, we cannot help but remind them of what Lenin said about this matter:

The experiences of all revolutionary movements show that the

---

1   *Al-Mar'at al-Yehudiyyah fi Filistin al-Muhtalah* [*Jewish Women in Occupied Palestine*], 75–6.

success of the revolution depends on the scope of female participation in it. The Soviet government undertakes everything that is in its powers to enable women to carry the burdens of socialist proletarian labor independently...the proletariat will not be able to achieve complete freedom until women achieve their full freedom.[1]

The question in essence, then, is not a question of leniency and condescension. From the socialist perspective, women form the greatest latent human reserve for the working class in general (country or city) in the Arab nation.

The incorporation of this reserve to its ranks will have in the end the most far-reaching effect on the cause of scientific socialism in our nation. From the social and human perspective, it is about the struggle to free half of the human element of Arab society from a truly frightening state of intellectual, moral, and material backwardness, about the freeing of these individuals from a terrifying despotic tradition that makes of women as human beings slave-girls who work in the home to look after and serve their owners, masters, and lords. We are not deceived by the appearances of external freedom alone in the manner of the freedom of "bourgeois dolls" and the like. For freedom has deeper and more profound meanings, meanings that can only be attained if the Arab woman becomes an effective and creative productive power in the life of Arab society and imposes herself on the traditional man on that basis. I do not know of a single contemporary society that believes itself worthy and deserving of being called socialist that can imagine that it can pull off one of its five-year plans, complete a large economic, industrial, or social project, or persevere in confronting the enemy until victory without the participation of the abilities of its female workers and the enlisting of them in the widest areas except for the Arab socialist societies.

It is widely believed that he who takes upon himself the duty of criticism is supposed to end by offering the solutions to the problems and predicaments he defines and crystallizes in his study. If the reader is still searching for an answer that can be detailed in two

---

1   *Lenin on the Emancipation of Women*, 58, 76.

or three pages, and he assumes that I can present him with what he conceives as the magic key that will save the Arab nation, with some almighty power, from its present ordeal, I assure him now that he is looking for the sort of answers and solutions that are the quickest route and the surest way to prolong the condition of defeat in our society and to firmly fix its premises and consequences. Although they do not name them as such, naturally, the Arab citizen – and even the Arab governments and regimes – often deploys these magic, rash solutions as a basis of his thinking.

As for more serious solutions, there has been no shortage of proposals, like the prompt union of the Arab states (the suggestions wavering between a comprehensive union and a federal union); a union among the states bordering Israel; a military union; Arab solidarity; economic mobilization; the placing of Arab oil and Arab financial power in the service of Arab causes in general and the Palestinian cause in particular; following scientific methods in propaganda, planning, etc.; the popular war of liberation; and so on. However, almost everyone proposing these solutions regards the possibilities of their achievement – even if partially – on the basis of a static view of the current Arab condition, of the existing political entities, and of accepting them as they are. Therefore, the call for the necessity of adhering to these solutions often becomes a type of missionary and rhetorical thinking because the advocates of the suggested solutions have yet to acknowledge that their call – with all that it includes of distinguished ideas if applied, and important and useful suggestions if carried out – is not a candidate for serious application and effective, continuous implementation as long as the Arab situation, the political entities, and dominant powers before the defeat are the same, in essence, as after the defeat. Observers of the current Arab condition are aware that the reactionary regimes have revived and are at ease after the defeat and that the revolutionary regimes are no longer capable of surpassing themselves to a higher and more advanced stage in their revolutionary and socialist character and in bold and effective leadership in order to create a comprehensive response to the Zionist occupation of Arab lands, old and new. As an example, let us look at what Walid Khalidi said in the course of defining the successful Arab strategy in this stage of resisting the occupation:

I admit that I cannot make sense of a serious strategy for resisting and defeating the Zionist danger that is not organically connected, intellectually and practically, to the principle of the total mobilization of all the Arab resources, on the basis of the coexistence of the Arab political entities and Arab elites, and that regards the Zionist danger as the first and most important priority on our present and future agenda until we attain victory.[1]

The principle of total mobilization of all Arab resources requires effective measures leading to, for example: 1) rendering Arab oil and Arab financial power effective (and deadly) weapons in the sum of Arab efforts 2) converting the Arab economy to a war economy, in effect 3) mobilizing the masses in a systematic and participatory manner in the battle (not its emotional mobilization in 24 hours via the media) 4) limiting foreign penetration in the economies and policies of many Arab states and even 5) building bunkers and fortifying cities, etc. If this is not the fundamental meaning of Walid Khalidi's principle of the mobilization of all Arab resources, then the principle at this time is merely formal, lacking content and application to the real world. Khalidi's appeal for the exercise of the principle of the total mobilization of all Arab resources remains reliant on a view that he restricts to the scope of the present "Arab political entities" and the ruling "Arab elites," and their coexistence. Does Walid Khalidi really imagine that the present "Arab political entities" and "Arab elites" that he talks about have the capability to adopt bold measures concerned with petroleum, mobilization, and money, etc. in order to give concrete form to the principle of the mobilization of all Arab resources? Is there anything in official or unofficial Arab behavior, during the war or after a year has passed, that indicates that the existing entities and elites are ready to adopt the principle of mobilization and fully apply the slogan to the confrontation?

Because Walid Khalidi's appeal to the principle of the mobilization of Arab resources does not consider the replacement of the

---

1   "Filistin 'Am 1968" ["Palestine Year 1968"] *Al-Thaqafat al-'Arabiyyah* [*Arab Culture*] (Beirut: July–August, 1968), 279.

previous entities and elites by a different type of "political entities" and "Arab elites," his appeal, although formally attractive and helpful, lacks effectiveness. For it lacks the ties with the kind of real situation that can transform it into act, application, and an implementation that accrues continuous and cumulative results.

Just as it was not possible to expect the Arab regimes that bore the responsibility for the defeat of 1948 to adopt effective measures for the mobilization of all Arab resources available at that time to resist and overcome the defeat, so likewise it appears to us that it is not at all realistic to expect the "Arab political entities" and "Arab elites" that bear responsibility for the defeat of 1967 to issue similar measures mobilizing all the Arab resources available today. There are clear reasons for this, connected with the class formation of the entities and elites mentioned, despite their diversity and differences, with the privileged interests that they typically represent, and with the capitalist economic ties that dominate them, and that make approximately 75 percent of the economy of the Arab nation a Western foreign economy from a practical perspective.

Most of these critical remarks also apply to the suggestions that Dr. Yusuf Sayegh presents in his book *Istratajiyyat al-'Aml l'-Tahrir Filistin* [*The Strategy of Action for the Liberation of Palestine*][1] and in his lecture "Al-Ta'b'al-Iqtisadiyyah wa'l-Nidal al-Qawmi" ["Economic Mobilization and the Nationalist Struggle"].[2] Here too we find that all his suggestions (very reasonable and useful in regards to principle) are erected on the assumption that the political entities, Arab regimes, and present leaderships will stay in place in regards to both their essence and foundations, and on the utopian hope that these entities will voluntarily adopt his suggestions (and others like them) and voluntarily implement them in an effective manner, motivated by patriotism and awareness of the Zionist danger! As an example, Dr. Sayegh, in the lecture mentioned above, urges the necessity of directing more Arab resources to defense, a necessary step, no doubt. However, Dr. Sayegh never raises the most important question, and that is what real guarantees do the Arab people possess that the additional money and resources

---

1 Dar al-Tali'ah [Vanguard Press], Beirut, 1968.
2 *Al-Thaqafat al-'Arabiyyah* [*Arab Culture*] magazine (July–August, 1968).

that he wants directed to the purposes of defense will lead to better results than the allocations to Arab defense have led to during the last twenty years, if it all takes place within the scope of the Arab condition preceding the defeat and with the oversight of the same "Arab elites" as before?

Dr. Sayegh says the following during another discussion on the Arab military leadership: "The flabbiness of the leaders was manifest, also, in their lack of acquaintance with the most recent military studies, and thus their intellectual powers were no longer honed."[1]

True and wise words. However, the mere introduction of some superficial adjustments to the military leadership so that the leaders pursue the most modern studies, and thus avoid flabbiness, will not remedy the deficiency. In reality, Dr. Sayegh's characterization of the military leadership is true of Arab society as a whole, since the great majority of the Arab doctors, lawyers, engineers, university professors, and professionals do not pursue the most modern studies in the areas of their specialties, or only rarely, and they are consequently afflicted by flabbiness and intellectual powers that have long lost their edge. This general, wide-ranging phenomenon cannot be remedied with the required swiftness, and before it is too late, by surrendering, with Dr. Sayegh and Walid Khalidi, to the existing Arab situation, the present "political entities" and the reigning "Arab elites," in the hope that the day will come when these entities will be convinced to take decisive measures to root out the bane of flabbiness in the life of Arab society. [2]

---

1   *Istratajiyyat al-'Aml l'-Tahrir Filistin* [*Strategy of Action for the Liberation of Palestine*], 15.

2   Naji 'Alloush summarized the meaning of this question completely and concisely in the following way: "What happened is a matter of destiny…a question of being or not being, and thus its meaning and significations should be exposed and clarified as such. In my view, it is a total collapse of systems, concepts, mentalities, strategies, and ways that have ruled this homeland of ours. If we consider what happened a 'setback' then I must believe in these systems, concepts and mentalities, etc., and in their ability to make a victory out of what happened. This is incompatible with primary indubitable axiomatic truths. If we consider what happened a relapse, we are among those who condemn themselves to blindness and are content with humiliation and shame as a fate." *Dirasah 'Arabiyyah* [*Arab Studies*] (July 1968), 10.

In other words, the Arabs will have to wait a long time for the eruption of new revolutionary powers from an Arab nation whose leadership becomes finally committed to the causes of the great majority of the individual members of the Arab people, that is, the causes
of the toiling masses and the interests of the working classes. I say
the Arabs will have to wait a long time because only this kind of
leadership will be capable of carrying the burdens of transforming
the deeds of the fedayeen into a real popular war of liberation in
which the mobilized masses participate effectively, of carrying the
burdens of proceeding down the difficult revolutionary road to win
the final Arab liberation from the dominance of colonialist economic interests and influence, and of achieving broad revolutionary changes pervading the life of Arab society in all aspects in order
to crush all the causes of impotence, weakness, and backwardness
that the successive Arab defeats have exposed. When the toiling
masses and Arab labor take up their own cause and go to battle
alongside their leaderships, it will be a real war, for then they will
be able to generate their own thinkers, writers, scientists, philoso-
phers, and dispense with our services and those of thinkers like us
who are not able to form – in virtue of the objective circumstances
– more than half-solutions on their behalf in a decisive transitional
historical stage.

Supplement

The following are some examples of what we said in the body of this study about the middle-roadism of Nasser's regime in Egypt. They are drawn from the writings and observations of some Egyptian thinkers.

"In other statistical reports published by the Central Office for Mobilization and Statistics in the United Arab Republic, the number of rural residents reached 17.7 million, and the number of them owning agricultural land whose surface exceeded five feddan was 178,000. If we assume that the number of those who are in free professions or officials living in rural areas amounts to twice this last number, then we find that there are more than 17 million in the rural areas who own nothing or less than five feddans. That is, that the peasants who rely on manual labor make up 60 percent of the total residents of the republic. If we add to this the manual workers and craftspeople in the cities, and their families, the percentage increases to more than 80 percent, at least. Despite this, we find that the share of the seats in elected political organizations that go to peasants and workers cannot drop below 50 percent, while, since the socialist state is a peasant and worker state, it ought not to drop below 80 percent. (From the Egyptian magazine *Al-Tali'ah* [*The Vanguard*], May 1968, 25.)

What follows is another note about the state of property in the United Arab Republic and the extent to which it falls short of the scientific socialist concept of the nature of property and the effect of this vacillation on the development and progress of the country: "If we leave the cities for the country, we are faced with numbers of greater meaning and significance. First, public property in land amounts to only 16 percent of the total arable land. As for the rest of the land, it is unfavorably fragmented. The number of those owning less than half a feddan is 1,459,167; the number of those owning a half to a whole feddan is 552,162; the number of those owning between one and two feddans is 327,612; and the number of those who own two to three feddans is 153,293...Those owning less than five feddans make up 94.5 percent of the total owners, possessing 57.1 percent of the land. That is, half the arable land in our country cannot employ under the current relations of production any modern agricultural methods, and when they are used, they will be extremely expensive and not profitable. Another third is distributed among rich landowners who possess three-quarters of the existing tractors in Egypt, and it is a capacity that suffices for more than what they own, to be sure, and they use them to take advantage of the small landowners. How is it, then, possible in a society that has been dominated until now by small-scale relations of production in agriculture, commerce, and, to some extent, manufacturing to apply modern methods of technology, science, and contemporary administration? The spread of the fragmentation of production not only damages production itself but also forms the social landscape for every deviation obstructing contemporary progress." (From the magazine *Al-Katib* [*The Writer*], May 1968, 29.)

Because of these fluid conditions that we are right to consider revolutionary in comparison to the conservatives and reactionaries, on the one hand, and conservative in comparison to the scientific socialists, on the other hand, startling things have occurred in the Egyptian countryside, where the peasant has found his gains stolen by exploitive rural groups. Kemal al-Din Rif'at explains this matter as follows: "However, the tyranny of feudalists reaches its full extent when they, for example, divest their property because of the imposition of sequestration. Despite this, they begin a capitalist life under almost feudal relations of production.

"The al-Faqi family in al-Manufiya had sequestration imposed on it in 1961. Despite this, it assessed its wealth in 1966 as double what it lost in 1961. It had changed from feudal to capitalist exploitation...the tyranny went so far that it was progressing each year with the help of its supporters in the villages and collusion with some employees of the agricultural reform, buying the livestock of the agricultural reform and fruit from the orchards that were placed under sequestration, at reduced prices, and reselling them at almost monopolistic prices...It had become clear that the reactionaries were ruling over the countryside, making from it a citadel for their anti-revolutionary movements, etc." ("Al-Tajribat al-Ishtirakiyyah fi'l-Jumhuriyyat al-'Arabiyyat al-Muttahida" ["The Socialist Experiment in the United Arab Republic"], a supplement to the magazine *Al-Katib* [*The Writer*], June 1967.)

We find another example of middle-roadism in the areas of political practice and organization in how the Arab Socialist Union was formed. This subject was raised as a question in Egypt in an urgent way after the proclamation of the program of March 30th because the Socialist Union in its formation, organization, and conception vacillated between an avant-garde political party and broad nationalist front without possessing the real advantages of either of these two extremes. The question proposed after the proclamation of March 30th and the changes it introduced into the organization of the Arab Socialist Union was: "Is the Socialist Union a party so that we are able to say that our country is witnessing the birth of a one-party system?...If the Socialist Union is not, then, one among other parties, then it is not possible to say that it is a nationalist or popular front or any form of a front because the front, as is well known, is equivalent to the convergence of numerous parties representing the interests of different classes, converging at a particular stage about a limited goal and program, and then breaking up after that in order to become narrower or wider according to the circumstances...The Socialist Union in its new version adopts the contents of the front without its form, that is, it is a quasi-front or collection of numerous classes and groups around one goal. However, the question remains whether this collection is a nationalist collection aiming at liberating the occupied territory and confronting the dangers that threaten independence, then breaking up and sending everyone on their own way and after their own class interests. (From the Egyptian magazine *Al-Tali'ah* [*The Vanguard*], May 1968, 143.)

Another example of middle-roadism in practice we take from the state of the press in Egypt. Jamal al-Sharghawi discussed this topic at length and with skill and precision in his article "Mulahathah 'ala Sihafat al-Sha'ab" ["Remarks on the People's Press"], where he explained that the press, on the one hand, is "a press of the people," and it is considered one of the organizations belonging to the Socialist Union as its property. On the other hand, we find that this press takes positions that are at variance with it and takes a path that brings it far from being the mouth of the Socialist Union, expressing its goals and message, supporting its activity, and spurring its development. That is, the press vacillates between the old inherited capitalist system and its real function as the press and property of the people in the stage of socialist revolution.

The writer of the article mentioned states: "The truly shocking thing is that our two large newspapers are, in fact, almost free of anything connected with workers...The two large newspapers take the same position in regards to the peasants. In regards to quantity, the two newspapers are almost free from anything about the peasants and nothing they publish goes beyond news concerning government decisions or the activity of organizations tied to the rural areas. That is, with what has no tie at all to the peasants themselves. The way our newspapers handle the activity of the Socialist Union never gives the activity prominence, and they do not put it in a place that makes it easy for the reader to see it. The news of the Socialist Union mostly comes secluded in a corner of the second newspaper in the section 'What Happened Outside of Cairo' and in the first in the section 'News' that is composed in 6-point and is almost unreadable. As for the first page, it only carries this news when there is something in it connected with very important national events or very prominent personalities. However, why does our press take this position remote from the basic capacities of the people, and from the political organization of the country? Moreover, why do the defects of the capitalist press persist despite all the years of revolution and despite the change in direction of our society towards socialism? We know that advertisement represents one of the most important sources of the financing of our press...A source of life for our press, then, is advertising. This is the beginning of the catastrophe, for only the press in capitalist countries depends on advertisement for financing, naturally...State financing can find its justification in that the press is a 'public servant of society', and financing through the Socialist Union can find its justification in that the press is an organ of political communication. However, what is the justification for financing by advertisement through the productive sector if this advertisement does not exercise a serious function in production? The problem here is to deduct a piece from the product of the producers to pay – in a non-productive manner – the press. In other words, the press, in reality, lives at the expense of the public sector: it is its parasite! This is not a reckless inference on our part, for all evidence confirms it." (The magazine *Al-Katib* [*The Writer*], June 1968, 73–89.)

Finally, another example taken from the public life in Egypt. "The truth is that no socialist state has witnessed the kind of competition for acquiring automobiles, refrigerators, and other means of luxury and comfort in the first years of socialist measures that is found among us, so that the spirit of flabbiness has pervaded the spirit of struggle, and aspiration for luxury the will to fight." (From the Egyptian magazine *Al-Tali'ah* [*The Vanguard*], August 1967, 28.)

RECEPTION
OF THE BOOK

I

Class Positioning in the Phenomenon of *Self-Criticism after the Defeat*

ELIAS SHAKIR

***Al-Tariq** [The Way]* **magazine, Beirut, June 1969**

When the Petty Bourgeoisie Criticizes Itself
In the first part[1] of this study, we reviewed some right-wing and bourgeois orientations that have contributed to "self-criticism" after the setback of the 5th of June, giving voice to either reactionary class perspectives entirely hostile to the liberation movement or idealist bourgeois intellectual perspectives unable to stand in the ranks of the liberation movement because of their narrow class views of the aggression and the motives behind it, and the goals it was and is trying to achieve.

We concluded that it is necessary, however, to distinguish between the criticism that is directed against the Arab movement of liberation, which is hostile to colonialism and possesses a social and economic content hostile to capitalism, aiming to strike down its progressive aspect, and the criticism spurred on by those who support the progressive achievements of the Arab movement for liberation in the face of the aggression in order to eliminate its effects and take the first step onto the road of liberation and socialism.

We have seen that bourgeois thought aspires to take advantage of the period following the aggression to blot out the organic

---

1   The writer, Elias Shakir, had already commented on some other books whose topic was the defeat, which is what is meant by "in the first part of this study, we reviewed..." *Self-Criticism after the Defeat* was not one of them. (Publisher's note)

relationship and common interests between the bourgeois class bound to the existence of the neocolonialist economy, especially the American one, and world imperialism and its chief military bases in the Middle East represented by Zionist colonialism in Palestine. Bourgeois thought takes aim, instead, at the interests and goals common to the Arab movement of liberation, the forces for socialism and freedom across the whole world, and at the friendship and alliance with the Soviet Union as the chief link to the position of resistance and confrontation.

As for emancipatory thought, it embarks from the positions of the popular classes who have the responsibility of protecting the movement of liberation and its progressive achievements from reactionary imperialist attacks, because it strives for liberation from the yoke of direct colonialism, neocolonialism, and the class colonialism practiced by the parasitic bourgeoisie, which has become a bridgehead and façade for neocolonialism.

***

The intellectual battle persisting after the aggression continues to revolve around giving the proper names to things and revealing the identity of the aggression, for popular struggles need clarity in their aims. When this clarity is achieved, they will be able to advance for the good of the movement for liberation with vigorous militancy as was confirmed in the experience of the struggle that took place in the short period since the aggression.

In this light, we turn to review two books concerned with "self-criticism," both commencing from the positions of the Arab movement for liberation and the confrontation with its enemies. We categorize these two books within nationalist emancipatory thought in its present phase of development in light of how they view the war of the Arab movement of liberation with American imperialism, in particular. Both books are published by the Dar al-Tali'ah [Vanguard Press] in Beirut, the first being *Self-Criticism after the Defeat* by Doctor Sadik Jalal al-Azm (now in its second printing), and the second, *From the Setback...to Revolution...* by Dr. Nadim al-Bitar.

In his book, Dr. Nadim al-Bitar repeats the following thought in several places, "the battle for the liberation of the occupied territories is merely one part of the total battle for those parts of the Arab nation where we confront the colonialism led by imperialist America everywhere. We must resist it in every fragment of this nation..." (p. 271) Dr. Sadik Jalal al-Azm voices the same thought with more clarity: "The deciding factor in determining America's Palestinian policy is the vital interests of America (in all their kinds) that extend to every corner of the world: the factors that ultimately determine its policy in Latin America and Vietnam also determine the pattern of its policies in the Middle East, where this policy takes on the shape of supporting Israel and the reactionary regimes and trying to fight all of the liberation movements that may have the audacity to eliminate American interests and threaten its security, stability, and expansion of influence." (p. 68, 69)

Indeed, this clarity concerning how American imperialism commences from its material economic interests is a suitable standard for distinguishing between those who stand in the ranks of the Arab movement for liberation and those who stand against it, without paying attention to who has attached himself to what ideology, with the knowledge that every ideological conception contains an expression of a specific class perspective. Indeed, the reactionary ideologies, which are therefore hostile to the movement for liberation, strive to erase the class character of the movement for liberation in this stage of its development in order to strip it of its effectiveness and in order that colonialism remains a metaphysical force that may be destroyed by fiery words and speeches. The forces of reaction attempt with their particular thinking and intellectual influence on the ranks of the revolutionary intellectuals who belong by a vast majority to the middle and petty bourgeois classes to divert the concern of the revolutionary forces away from the necessity of striking the imperialist monopolist material interests in every liberated state because this goal entails a collision with the classes tied economically, and thus intellectually, with the imperialists and the removal of these classes from the positions of power.

This class aspect of the movement for liberation is not absent from the thought of Sadik Jalal al-Azm and Nadim al-Bitar, as a result of their commitment to total liberation. Sadik Jalal al-Azm calls for the necessity "in the end for the toiling masses and the interest of the working class" to "carry the burdens of proceeding down the difficult revolutionary road to win the final Arab liberation from the dominance of colonialist economic interests and influence..." (p. 166) As he says in his discussion of the thought of Dr. Hasan Sa'ab, "the chief matter that ought to be the focus of our intellectual and scientific concerns is scientific socialism in itself" and he describes middle-roadism in thinking as "tricks that aim to falsify the situation and distort the serious attempts to understand it and the role of the Arab left in regards to it." (p. 136) As for Dr. Nadim Bitar, he states in his discussion of the thought of Dr. Constantin Zureiq, who called for rejecting class struggle: "The nationalist call stumbled – if this is true – not because it practiced class struggle, but because it came late to practicing it, and because it practiced it with reluctance." (p. 97)

Right-wing thought strives to erase the economic and social content of the Arab movement of liberation, and this erasure amounts to a blow against the foundations of the movement of liberation. However, the real issue is not about whether the movement of liberation has an economic and social content, but rather how to define its content.

There has never been a political movement without a social and economic content, without class content, for the class struggle is what motivates history. When idealist bourgeois thinking tries to isolate Arab nationalism as a concept from social and economic content, that is, when it makes it a struggle in thought only, among some thinkers from the "elect" that are the motor of history, its aim is to hide the class interests of the ruling bourgeoisie. For these interests clash essentially not only with the class interests of the workers and the indigent peasantry but also with the necessity of total and final liberation from colonialism. We have already observed this in the analysis of some of the models of idealist right-wing thought in the first part of this study.

This is why the statement that Arab nationalism has a social and economic content does not suffice. We must give content to the notion that liberation from colonialism entails a transformation of the current economic and social system. This transformation, and the simultaneous liberation from colonialism, can only be completed in a socialism that imposes itself as the goal and ideology of the movement for liberation, for objective reasons. The most important is that the transformation of the social and economic system is a class struggle against the bourgeoisie undertaken by the popular masses, and whose socialist horizon becomes clear to these masses with the accumulation of struggles for the sake of political independence and secession from the regions of influence of the neocolonialists. This occurs within the scope of a world transformation from capitalism to socialism, with the deepening of the world imperialist contradictions and the increasing of capitalist aggressiveness as the highest stage of capitalism, so that the hidden neocolonialism loses the cover that enabled it to deceive the masses and conceal itself behind "patriotic" fronts.

The socialist horizon emerges with the persistence of the struggle of the popular classes for their vital demands against the background of the increasing effectiveness of the socialist model in both solving social problems and providing for the spiritual and material needs of the people, along with the proofs of its superiority to idealist bourgeois thought in solving the most important and most complicated matters of contemporary culture.

This success enables it to attract wide sectors of the educated in different fields of science, art, and literature so that it has become difficult for one to presume the respect of the people for him as an intellectual if he lacks acquaintance with Marx from the original sources. When we look to the "self-criticism" that commences from positions of the movement for liberation, it is inevitable that we evaluate this criticism in the light of the standards of the movement for liberation itself at the level that it has reached, and this requires the determining of the standards of evaluation, so that we can shift after that to treating some issues that the books of Sadik Jalal al-Azm and Nadim al-Bitar raise, without being able to perform a comprehensive view of their two books.

The first standard that suggests itself is the benefit to the present state of the movement for national liberation and the real possibilities of its development: this guarantees that we do not stray from reality and fall into subjective arbitrariness.

The second standard is scientific socialism as a method for analyzing from the perspective of the working class (the most revolutionary class in the alliance of classes and groups that aspire to total liberation) and as a revolutionary theory that aids us in steering clear of despairing defeatist positivism. In fact, the distinction between the two standards is only apparent, for scientific socialism requires taking into consideration the state of national liberation as an objective movement. Similarly, the movement for liberation summons scientific socialism as a matter of history and necessity as its theory, with the altering of the balance of powers at the global level in favor of socialism, with the increase in the weight and role of the working classes within the movement for liberation, and with the clarifying of the essence of liberation from colonialism as the socio-economic transformation of the society that still relies on the relations of capitalist production developing within the framework of dependency on the world imperialist monopolies.

Dr. Sadik Jalal al-Azm joins Dr. Nadim al-Bitar in criticizing many negative aspects in the progressive Arab regimes that were the chief target of the war begun by the imperialists by means of Israel on the Arab movement for liberation. Dr. Nadim al-Bitar says in this regard: "I repeat that the primary goal of the American imperialists and Israel in the June War was to kill the Revolution of July 23rd because of the role it plays as the base of the Arab movement for liberation." (p. 295)

In fact, how both books concentrate, like many others, on criticizing the experiment of the United Arab Republic certainly goes back to the leading role that this revolution plays in the Arab movement for liberation. The source of this assessment is not subjective, but a matter of conviction for both its enemies and friends, for a number of reasons, the most important of which are the following: a) the centrality of Egypt and its demographic, economic, and strategic weight in the Arab world; b) the perseverance of Egypt's experience of liberation in the face of imperialist conspiracies against the Third World in general, so that it has become an important model for those who want to study the case of liberation despite the particularity of its own circumstances.

We have seen in the first part of this study, relying on a document published by the Arab Socialist Union, that the regime in the UAR was not socialist. It is important to remember that these documents and declarations published by the Arab Socialist Union proclaim that socialism is the goal of the revolution.

Despite (1) that the state and the public sector in the UAR dominate "the whole system of credit, banks, and transport services, and 85 percent of the means of industrial production," (2) that the state and Socialist Union stand resolutely at the side of the peasants in their struggle with the previous owners of the land included in agricultural reform, and (3) that the intellectual discussion that accompanies social planning and reform takes place in the name of socialism, it is not possible to say that the revolution has become a socialist revolution. This is confirmed by the declarations of the leaders of the UAR themselves, and this is consistent with the class nature of authority and the official ideology that justifies this authority.

There is a firm connection between the statement of Kemal al-Din Rif'at that the state "is a state for a number of revolutionary classes" and his statement that "accordingly, it is not scientific socialism in its Marxist meanings, but, in any case, merely shares some of its characteristics."

The connection between these two citations results from the relation of the infrastructure of society in the UAR to its ideological superstructure.

The statement, then, that political authority in the UAR is in the hands of the petty bourgeoisie is not an indictment directed at this authority, but it is required by scientific socialism as a method for thought and application. In the study mentioned above, Kemal al-Din Rif'at acknowledges the nature of this authority when he divides the movement for liberation into three stages, the first under the leadership of "patriotic capitalism," the second under the leadership of "petty capitalism" and the intellectuals it has drawn from the revolutionary intelligentsia. As for the third socialist stage, it will be led by the working class. He makes clear that the first stage has expired and the third stage is yet to arrive. We then are in the second stage under the leadership of the petty bourgeoisie, and we cannot consider the authority in this case a socialist authority as long as the working class continues to be far from eading the "alliance of the forces of the working people" and despite that the present leadership solidifies the role of the present workers in this alliance and their leading role in the socialist future.

The class alliance of the forces of the "working people," and the composition of workers, peasants, and medium and petty patriotic capitalists under the leadership of the petty bourgeoisie and its intellectuals, who wage class battle against the client classes in the circumstances of oppressed nationalities liberated from colonialism, is an alliance that has acknowledged the presence of class struggle directed against the agents of colonialism. However, it tries to freeze this struggle internally, relying for this on the ideology of an accommodating "middle-roadism." Sadik Jalal al-Azm describes this as "fluid conditions that we are right to consider revolutionary in comparison to the conservatives and reactionaries, on the one hand, and conservative in comparison to the scientific socialists, on the other hand." (p. 169)

He says "moreover, that generated the obvious truth that the freezing of Arab politics within the limits of applying slogans that initially make their case negatively, like 'a non-capitalist road,' 'positive neutrality,' 'non-alignment,' and 'the Third World' (which is supposed to mediate between the first and second world) will lead to crippling of revolutionary Arab politics in its confrontation with the existing Zionist challenge, no matter at what level we want this confrontation to take place, whatever the circumstances." (p.142)

These slogans that the author criticizes in the name of scientific socialism and names "middle-roadism" are slogans that express the ideology of the petty bourgeoisie and their beatific dreams of a society resting on the reconciliation of the classes. Scientific socialist thought arose and was developed in the hands of Marx, Engels, and Lenin with the critique of similar petty bourgeois thinking in order to remove its influence from the working class that was not able to unite, achieve class-consciousness, and seize power until freed from the effect of petty bourgeois ideas and illusions.

Therefore, the Arab socialists must wage a long struggle against this "middle-roadism" in thinking and not to efface secondary contradictions within the class base of the revolution of liberation (the primary contradiction being between it and the class tied to neo-colonialism) if they are serious in their commitment to pursue the revolution of national liberation to its end.

* * *

Indeed, petty bourgeois socialist thinking in the UAR is in this area much franker about its petty bourgeois character than some of those who criticize it from the left. For it acknowledges that socialism means the working class taking the leadership of the "alliance of the forces of the working people." This is, no doubt, the result of the change of the balance of power in favor of the working class within the current class alliance. However, despite this, they continue to offer a wide variety of justifications for the failure of the workers and peasants to attain a role in the leadership that matches their real importance in production.

This is reflected at the ideological level. Dr. Sadik Jalal al-Azm states: "This middle-roadism was even reflected in the circles that are supposed to represent the Arab scientific socialist left in the United Arab Republic, and there are some who spread, rationalize, and give it a philosophical veneer to the point where a group there has emerged from this left with a novel, strange, odd composition, its name being the socialist-scientific-Islamic-fideistic party." (p. 138)

How does this petty bourgeois accommodation look in practice?

Kemal al-Din Rifa't states: "The unification of the socialist forces is considered the chief link in the political standpoint, when this unity is simultaneously the building of the desired political organization" (the appendix to *Al-Katib* [*The Writer*] magazine, May 1967). The socialist forces alluded to is "the alliance of forces of the working people," that is, classes who stand in contradiction and conflict, even if they are secondary contradictions at the present stage. The unification of forces like these under the motto of the socialism that we call "scientific" entails the working class renouncing its leading role in favor of the petty bourgeoisie. This is justified by stating that the peasant masses and petty bourgeoisie are not yet convinced that the working class should take a leading role. However, this is inconsistent with how the popular masses have endorsed the socialist mottos, especially the motto that passes off socialist democracy as a quasi-parliamentary bourgeois democracy in which the workers and peasants have attained 51 percent of the seats in the leading organizations, when they have the right to much more than this by the standards of bourgeois democracy itself. At present, they have not even attained the nominal proportion dedicated to them because of the elastic definitions of the workers and the peasantry, and because of the dominance of the state apparatuses inherited from capitalist and feudal institutions in implementing "socialist" decisions.

In such a situation, even acknowledgments of secondary contradictions between the "forces of working people" are insufficient. As Kemal al-Din Rif'at stated in the document cited above: "It is not improbable that non-antagonistic contradictions between the popular forces will become antagonistic," whether because one of the classes errs by accident or strays intentionally from the "path of socialism."

What do these words mean? Who judges whether this or that class has strayed? Can the path of socialism be anything other than the struggle of the working class for the leadership of popular alliance? Lenin says:

> Like everything else in the world, the revolutionary-democratic dictatorship of the proletariat and the peasantry has a past and a future. Its past is autocracy, serfdom, monarchy and privilege. In the struggle against this past, in the struggle against counterrevolution, a "single will" of the proletariat and the peasantry is possible, for here there is unity of interests. Its future is the struggle against private property, the struggle of the wage worker against the employer, the struggle for socialism. Here singleness of will is impossible. Here our path lies not from autocracy to a republic but from a petty-bourgeois democratic republic to socialism.
>
> The time will come when the struggle against the Russian autocracy will end and the period of democratic revolution will be over in Russia; then it will be ridiculous to talk about the "singleness of will" of the proletariat and the peasantry, about a democratic dictatorship, etc. When that time comes, we shall attend directly to the question of the socialist dictatorship of the proletariat and deal with it at greater length.
>
> However, at present, the party of the advanced class cannot but strive most energetically for a decisive victory of the democratic revolution over tsarism. And a decisive victory means nothing else than the revolutionary-democratic dictatorship of the proletariat and the peasantry. (Lenin, *Two Tactics of Social-Democracy in the Democratic Revolution*)

If we view in this light authority in the UAR, we are able to say that the petty bourgeois leadership of the alliance of the forces of the working people imposes a number of compromises on the working classes. In the nature of things, the time has not yet arrived for the discussion of socialism as an existing system. The basic task is still the achieving of the complete victory of the democratic revolution that, within the circumstances of the UAR, is a revolution of liberation against colonialism. The aggression of the 5th of June targeted the hopes of the Arabs for liberation and unity, but although it was a nationalist aggression, it was also a counterrevolution in which, intentionally or unintentionally, sectors of the petty bourgeoisie benefited from their positions in the state apparatus to create privileges for themselves. These interests are incompatible with the interests of the vast popular majority of workers, indigent peasants, and segments of the petty bourgeoisie in bringing the revolution of liberation to total victory.

Scientific socialism, then, acts decisively in exposing and combating bourgeois interests incompatible with the requirements of social transformation for the sake of total liberation. However, at the same time it addresses the facts of relative class forces not only in terms of numbers but also in terms of organization and consciousness. For political organization and scientific consciousness both play the fundamental role in socialist transformation. What also plays an important role in this area is criticism of the vague petty bourgeois concepts that enable the infiltration of capitalist counterrevolutionary forces into the ranks of the revolution, crippling and sabotaging it, as occurred before, during, and after the aggression of the 5th of June. Exposing "middle-roadism" as Sadik Jalal al-Azm has done is necessary. However, such criticism is defective if it stops with appearances without distinguishing between the conflicting forces within the ranks of the revolution behind the façade of stability, calm, and fabricated mutual support between the classes. Although the aggression has failed in overthrowing the progressive regimes, we must remember that it has taken on other forms internally amidst the harsh setback that has befallen the progressive forces. Dr. Sadik Jalal al-Azm states: "the reactionary regimes have revived and are pleased after the defeat [*this is true, author's interjection*]. The revolutionary regimes are no longer capable of surpassing themselves to a higher and more advanced stage in their revolutionary and socialist character and in bold and effective leadership in order to create a comprehensive response to the Zionist occupation of Arab lands, old and new." (p. 161) The second part of the conclusion requires some discussion, for Dr. al-Azm imagines the situation as if the task proposed right now before the socialist forces is the overthrow of these regimes and their replacement by more revolutionary regimes. If it is true that we must assume this goal – and there are those who proclaim it publicly – this is a call to undertake an adventure in circumstances that Dr. al-Azm himself admits are inclined in favor of the reactionaries who have revived since the 5th of June. This plan conflicts with the plan of perseverance in the face of the attack of colonialism and counterrevolution, which the masses assumed in their powerful direct intervention upon hearing of the resignation of Nasser. Therefore, every position that commences with impatience – and impatience is one of the characteristics of the petty bourgeoisie – aids the revived counterrevolution in dispersing the forces of revolution. Every adventure in these circumstances is necessarily a desperate, futile adventure because it does not take the desire of the masses into consideration.

The broadening and extending of the Palestinian resistance and the activities of the fedayeen are nothing but an expression of this will to perseverance: nothing else is needed for its explanation. The fault that might be attributed to Dr. Sadik Jalal al-Azm is, then, the lack of scientific socialist reflection on the balance of class forces within the ranks of an emancipatory revolution that is not yet a socialist revolution and which cannot be considered one even if it claims that for itself, given that the revolution in Egypt does not claim that it has begun the building of socialism, even if it gives socialist names to petty bourgeois democratic reforms. Criticisms like these continue to be external and marginal to the battle of perseverance against the counterrevolutionary forces. The internal battle in the UAR has involved, both before and after the 5th of June, the formation of the political apparatus for the revolution within the apparatuses of the Socialist Union. Indeed, the building of a socialist political apparatus committed to the transformation of society in accord with the socialist revolution cannot be accomplished except by achieving a decisive victory over the counterrevolutionary forces, and it is possible to complete this by means of the stance of perseverance itself so that perseverance becomes the measure of the revolutionary and counterrevolutionary forces. Therefore, perseverance is a transformative perseverance that culls out from the ranks of revolution the forces who want to abandon the trenches and retreat in defeat from those who exit the trenches to rush with courage to the front. It is the petty bourgeoisie that leaves its positions because of their discordant natures, reluctance, and smallness of spirit.

The lack of scientific precision in determining the stage of the Arab revolution and the class forces that compete for its leadership appears also in the criticism of the "social personality that the inherited Arab milieu instilled and developed in each of us," in the words of Dr. al-Azm. This lack of precision is concealed in his ignoring that scientific socialism does not look to the person as an absolute essence but as the result of class-based social relations determining his behavior according to his position in the relations of production, and as a historical result of the development of the forces and relations of production in each state of its development.

Dr. al-Azm gives to this Arab personality in a general way the name "the clever personality," borrowing this name from the study of Dr. Hammed Ammar by the name of *Fi Bina' al-Bashir: Dirasah fi'l-Taghyir al-Hadari wa'l-Fikr al-Tarbawi* [*On Building Human Beings: Studies in Cultural Change and Educational Thought*]. Among the characteristics of this personality, for example, are "the constant search for the shortest and fastest route to realize particular goals and aims while avoiding the toil and the effort usually required in overcoming impediments to reach this goal, and avoiding using the natural means to attain it." (p. 70) On the one hand, the author qualifies himself by saying: "The clever personality is nothing but an abstraction and pattern, and does not exist in living reality except in the shape of characteristics, patterns of behavior, reactions, and sensibilities that describe individuals in a specific social environment and to different degrees, sometimes increasing, sometimes decreasing, from one individual to another according to circumstances and conditions." On the other hand, he does not limit the application of this abstraction and pattern to the petty bourgeoisie, which naturally provides the model of the society in which it is the dominant class. For identifying this affiliation and its consciousness is absolutely necessary so that the petty bourgeois individual can transcend his reality and emulate the persevering worker instead of chasing the fugitive hope that he emerges from his existential and psychological crisis into the luxuries of the children of the capitalist class wallowing in rank and wealth. This is the source of the tendency of this kind of individual "to sudden enthusiasm, extreme boldness, and scoffing at difficulties at the beginning of the road, then indifference and apathy when the clever personality realizes that the matter calls for steadfastness, perseverance, and systematic action, and that the results will only emerge slowly and cumulatively." (p. 75)

Likewise, the statement that "the Arab revolutionary youth today is a political revolutionary but, in the depths of his heart, he is usually a social, religious, cultural, ethical, and economic conservative " (p. 78) applies absolutely to the petty bourgeois individual. However, likewise, all criticism at this level without a clear qualification as to class remains idealist and moralistic even if it is made in the name of socialism.

The criticism of Dr. Nadim al-Bitar is in the same mold, because when he criticizes ideological, psychological, and conceptual deviations among the Arab revolutionaries he does not distinguish the class affiliations of these revolutionaries. For there are petty bourgeois revolutionary intellectuals just as there are revolutionary intellectuals who are aware of the hazards into which their bourgeois class origins pull them and try to avoid these hazards through constant self-criticism. Dr. Nadim al-Bitar states in his marginal remarks on page 256 of his book: "The American barbarism and its instrument Israel cannot increase in power. All they are able to do is transfer a part of their power from one place to another, that is, from America to the occupied territories. However, we increase in power year after year. The power we attain entails a weakness for our enemies, whose weakness increases with our strength. All that we need is the correction of the Arab self and the time to benefit from our tremendous latent powers."

The raising of the issue in this form does not surpass the petty bourgeois view of the battle with "American barbarism" although it cites Marx, Lenin, and the socialist thinkers alongside the bourgeois thinkers. For when Dr. al-Bitar presents a cascade of citations from socialist books in order to stress the subjective factor, he does this to convince those who neglect this side of "the Marxisants," just as he says. However, he gives no indication that the basic condition for the growth of socialist consciousness of the working class is the existence of a political party dedicated to this class, whose strategy includes the task of seizing political power. The pursuit of class conflict does not happen automatically, but manifests itself with the greatest clarity in the shift from the economic struggle to the political struggle and the joining of the two struggles with the goal of achieving power. The criticism that Dr. Nadim al-Bitar pursues in this area resembles that of ordinary people in our country who explain every social disaster by saying "we Arabs are selfish" or "we Arabs do not love one another" or other expressions of self-rebuke that reveal a total ignorance of the class struggle.

Indeed, the presumption that what we lack is a revolution of the self presumes at the same time that the economic transformations in the progressive regimes amount to socialist transformations, and thus that all we still need is a revolution of the self. This is far from the truth. In the view of the author, the revolutions of the self require more than economic reforms, they require a battle that purifies the traditional Arab self inherited from our backward societies, a transformation that "socialism" is unable to provide because of its ideological and conceptual deviations. The United States of America provides us this battle by waging an unending war on us and on our goals of unity, and the answer to its challenge is the immediate unification of the revolutionary regimes: "with time, independent revolutionary entities create for themselves – if the ideological, psychological, and revolutionary conditions that crystallize in the resolute desire for unity which is nourished by revolutionary commitment do not accompany it – an independent, local tradition that becomes hard to supersede or negate after it continues past a certain point. For whenever the date for the unification of the revolutionary regimes is postponed, the obstacles to this unification increases. Therefore, the immediate unification of these revolutionary regimes is the major effective tool to avoid... Balkanization. The dissolution that afflicted the union between Syria and Egypt provides an example of great clarity for what I mean, for everything that is said to the effect that the source of the dissolution was objectively necessary indicates either ignorance or a defeatist mentality. Certainly, there were objective forces that rejected the unification and acted to destroy it: But what unification does not encounter similar forces? Human weakness among the revolutionaries facilitated this deed, because those working for unification themselves were not transformed by true moral, voluntary, psychological, intellectual, revolutionary attributes, because the majority of them did not know anything about revolutionary authenticity, and because human smallness characterized so many of them." (p. 249)

It is clear, then, that he gives moral conditions priority over objective circumstances for the completing of the unification. In addition, it suggests a lack of scientific certainty concerning that Arab nationalist unity is a response to certain objective conditions.

This critique is more scientifically defective than Gamal Abdel Nasser's self-criticism after the secession, when he said that one of its chief causes was the lack of consideration of the conflicting class interests in a single organization (the nationalist union, at that time). Thus the victor in the struggle was the class that was economically stronger, the capitalist-feudal class bound economically to imperialism, which was the target of economic reforms during the unification.

The author takes the same moralistic position on the issue of socialism, saying: "The objective transformations we undergo and the tendencies that guide them induce, for example, a socialist solution [*note how he neglects the internal class battle that ends in the socialist solution to the benefit of the working class, author's interjection*], but this does not mean that this solution appears automatically, or else why is there any need to call for a revolutionary socialist solution, and thus we fall into the same error into which the reformist democratic socialist movement fell, an error that in our present stage entails the rejection of socialism. For the objective transformations do not determine how we arrive at socialism, its nature, its means, the degree to which it has been achieved, its effectiveness, etc.: All of these are linked to the kind of intellectual and psychological dimensions that accompany it." (p. 248) Here we see again that the basic condition is a moralistic one, and that the internal class structure of the "forces of the working people" is neglected, this structure in which capitalism plays a fundamental role, even if under the supervision of the "petty bourgeois intellectuals." For we know that the capitalist intellectuals possess wide experience in speaking in a language that enchants the petty bourgeoisie, that they inhabit distinguished positions in the state institutions, and that they remain in these positions with changes in regime. With their long experience, they are able to infiltrate and dominate the "alliance of the forces of the working people" and turn reforms to the benefit of their class, profiting from the absence of representatives of the working class and the paralysis of its independent institutions.

Depriving the class struggle of its real place in raising the consciousness of the masses can lead the progressive regimes to the sort of failures that befell the unity of Syria and Egypt and to counter-revolutionary coup d'état.

On this topic, neither book mentions the role that the counter-revolutionaries played in the defeat of the 5th of June, which would have destroyed the regimes if not for the intervention of the masses and the support of socialists in the Arab world and the world-at-large. This support became an inducement for criticism on the part of some of the petty bourgeois intellectuals and their organizations, who were pushed by defeat to infantile emotional positions, under the pretense that the support of the progressive regimes on the part of socialists is to be considered a reformist position. For these regimes are no longer able to make further progress towards socialism and have become unable even to "remove the effects of the aggression." Dr. Nadim al-Bitar agrees with Dr. Sadik Jalal al-Azm in this estimation, saying: "The republic became unable after the defeat (as it was before it)...to play the role of base [*for the Arab revolution, author's interjection*], which was until now its role. The need to construct a union between it, Syria, Iraq, and Algeria increases in intensity and urgency. I am not able to do anything here but issue a warning that the lack of speed in realizing this base, ignoring it or making plans in a different direction, will not lead to the establishing of another base but the opposite result and this is the deepening of the divisions." (p. 294)

He supports this demand by presuming that "Abdel Nasser was

until last May (1967) devoting all his efforts to delay a direct battle with Israel and to concentrate on the social revolution in the other Arab regions as a path to this battle." (p. 288) However, documents from the United Arab Republic confirm that for Egypt, just as Kemal al-Din Rif'at stated in May 1967 at the Socialist conference in Algeria, the chief task was building a political apparatus, a battle that has yet to be decided. However, Abdel Nasser's position on unity was built on, especially after the experience of the secession, not imposing it by might or intervention but leaving its completion to objective circumstances and the free popular will that Dr. al-Bitar counts as second to the moralistic psychological conditions of the leaders. While Dr. Nadim al-Bitar refers to the operation of the United Arab Republic in Yemen (p. 295), this was not about imposing revolution on Yemen but supporting the democratic revolution against the foreign imperialist reactionary attack. Indeed, the shifting of attention away from the internal battle occurring with the forces of the counterrevolution that the objective capitalist development has mustered inside the "Alliance of the Forces of the Working People," whether before or after the defeat, only serves the counterrevolution. The call for immediate unification in these circumstances depends on, as Dr. Sadik al-Azm states, a "static view of the current Arab condition, of the existing political entities, and of accepting them as they are. Therefore, the call for the necessity of adhering to these solutions often becomes a type of missionary and rhetorical thinking because the advocates of the suggested solutions have yet to acknowledge that their call – with all that it includes of distinguished ideas if applied, and important and useful suggestions if carried out – is not a candidate for serious application and effective, continuous implementation as long as the Arab situation, the political entities, and dominant powers before the defeat are the same, in essence, as after the defeat." (p. 160, 161)

In general, petty bourgeois thought commences from ideological representations of unity: the unity of regions, the unity of classes, the unity of ideologies, and this as a reaction to the crises that it suffers as a result of individual fragmentation. This collides with individualism in itself and this is its tragedy. Petty bourgeois individualism rests on the dissolution of differences and rounding of corners until it is stricken by despair, and then it shifts to emotional explosions that it tries to pass on, in turn, to the working class in order to draw it into anarchic positions and away from the plan of patient persistent struggle, by simplifying scientific socialism and attempting to apply it in a mechanical manner resting on delusions.

When the regime in the UAR states that it possesses a special scientific socialism that is non-Marxist under the pretext that Arab socialism is not incompatible with religion while Marxism is atheistic, and when Kemal al-Din Rif'at states that "according to this, scientific socialism does not have the meaning of Marxism, but it is, in any case, one of the attributes of Marxism," it is as if it was suggested that socialism is scientific and something else and that this something else is in Egypt not what it is in Marxism. This talk reflects in reality the thinking of the class dominating "The Alliance of the Forces of the Working People," and, in periods of increasing class tension, it plays the roles of both foe and arbitrator in regards to the working class.

The same class departure point prompts Dr. al-Bitar to state: "I am not a Marxist...However, this does not mean I reject Marxism and curse it: No, not at all – I, in fact, employ it as one of the few great social philosophies that modern social science has begot." (p. 94)

The introduction of Marxism into the petty bourgeois eclecticism has its source, as we saw, in its need to depend on the working classes and attempt to seize their support in the battle against capitalism and feudalism, just as it has its source in the shift in the balance of powers across the world to the benefit of the socialists, so that it becomes difficult for an intellectual to be called progressive and revolutionary if he is hostile to Marxism. These are some of the bases for the appearance of modern revisionisms.

However, despite this, when it is a battle between the progressive regimes and the counterrevolutionaries, as is the case now, Marxism is on the side of the progressive regimes, decisively and without reluctance, in contrast to many positions within the petty bourgeoisie that turn against their regimes from the right and from the left because of their despair, emotionality, lack of spirit, or desire to maintain their privileges.

Indeed, the position of Dr. Nadim al-Bitar, for example, at least theoretically, represents a step backward in what relates to the regime in the UAR. Dr. Sadik Jalal al-Azm has recognized this slip and proclaims at the end of his book that individual intellectuals "are not able to form – in virtue of the objective circumstances – more than half solutions on their behalf in a decisive transitional historical stage." (p.166)

Moreover, the progressive revolution in Egypt presents a democratic revolution that is yet to finally defeat the forces of reactionary counterrevolution, and it is therefore deserving of support, just as Lenin says. It is also an emancipatory nationalist revolution calling on the Leninist Internationale to support it with the entirety of its means until it achieves total victory over the imperialist bases and their dangers. Lenin said concerning this:

> The social revolution can come only in the form of an epoch in which are combined civil war by the proletariat against the bourgeoisie in the advanced countries and a whole series of democratic and revolutionary movements, including the national liberation movement, in the undeveloped, backward and oppressed nations.
>
> Why? Because capitalism develops unevenly, and objective reality gives us highly developed capitalist nations side by side with a number of economically slightly developed, or totally undeveloped, nations.

As for the obligation to transform society to socialism, it will necessarily be completed because total liberation and total economic independence for states undergoing liberation cannot be accomplished except through socialist transformation. Socialist transformation is a daily struggle which involves the tasks of emancipatory revolution, democratic revolution, and socialist revolution. Any reluctance to waging the daily class struggle and the popular struggle against colonialism, however it covers itself with the mottos of "revolution" demanding everything or nothing, abandons not only socialism but national liberation too. When the time of socialist revolution comes – and no one can pretend to predict the date – "we will discuss the details," as Lenin said.

Criticism of the Criticism of
Dr. Sadik Jalal al-Azm

GHASSAN KANAFANI

Al-Sayad magazine, Beirut, October 24, 1968

After the Arab revolution entered a number of crises and reversals, the art of self-criticism began to flourish greatly, self-criticism
becoming almost a fashion in the age of reversals, everyone dab-
bling in it without reluctance or limit in an unhappy attempt to
cleanse the conscience from the errors and lapses of the past.

Some of those practicing self-criticism sometimes resort to it to
convince the masses that "the past is dead" and that they are today
something different than they were yesterday. Accordingly, it is
obligatory to trust them again so that they can work the wonder of
surpassing themselves, transcending objective reality despite how
weak and emaciated they appear.

Self-mourning
In order to persuade the masses of the veracity of the desire to transcend the errors of the past, the self-critic overstates his critique to
the point where it becomes something more like "self-mourning"
or "self-lamenting" so that everything objective and definite is lost
in it, and it is immersed in the desire to "bluff" the citizens, and
influence them through raw dramatic exaggerations.

There are other groups that practice criticism and self-criticism
to direct suspicion away from themselves and towards others. This
kind of critic certainly knows that he is not free of the suspicion

that the others cast but throws it in the face of his enemies in order to turn attention from his errors and faults. These "critics" lose the advantage of self-criticism in the depths of the political struggles and propaganda campaigns that, most of the time, make a victim of pure objective truth.

The use of self-criticism for these purposes leads, in the end, to its losing its significance as one of the means in the scientific inquiry that aspires to uncover errors and defects in the project of the Arab revolution – in its regimes, movements, and currents – and as a means to ascertaining the causes and factors that allow it to fall into these errors. In so doing, it leads the Arab revolution, or any movement of confrontation, out of the crises in which they have fallen.

Rehabilitation

In trying to rehabilitate self-criticism, and to free it from the blemishes that surround it as a result of its submitting to the standards of partisan political interests, the young thinker Dr. Sadik Jalal al-Azm undertook to compose the book *Self-Criticism after the Defeat*, and he has introduced his book by stating, "I hope that enlightened Arab thinking will have surpassed the stage in which criticism is considered merely the activity of disparagement or the unending enumeration of defects, faults, and shortcomings. In other words, that it will have achieved a level capable of considering criticism the precise analysis that identifies weak spots, sources of helplessness, and influences that have lead to the existence of faults and shortcomings."

Unless conscious Arab thought has reached the level that al-Azm demands of it, then what he presents in his book should be considered, no doubt, an attempt to achieve this goal. To what extent does al-Azm succeed in this attempt? We shall commence with a discussion of some of the book's contents and its chief ideas.

The Way to Salvation

Dr. al-Azm devotes the greater part of his book to discuss the positions and faulty analyses that some Arab thinkers and decision-makers have undertaken in determining the causes of the defeat of the 5th of June. He applies the scalpel of dissection and criticism against the metaphysical explanations that attribute the defeat to the angry heavens or to accidental factors, and he refuses to explain the defeat in terms of Israeli treachery or colonialist intervention.

The defeat, in his view, has one cause and that is the backwardness of Arab society, its being trapped in the frame of primitive human relations that are dominated by indifference, superstition, traditionalism, and an aversion to real change that releases the powers and creative possibilities of the masses. He, then, believes that exploding the foundations of backwardness in Arab society is the way to salvation, and that this task falls to the Arab revolutionary alone.

> The gist of the account is that the forces of revolution in the Arab nation, and especially in the more progressive Arab countries, must now more than ever strive to introduce the Arab nation into the realm of the twentieth century, in its science, planning, industry, economy, and technical process, by adopting firmly and decisively modern science and technology, and giving both priority and precedence in economic, social, and cultural planning.

Dr. Al-Azm rejects what has been circulated by some right-wing and technocratic circles, that it is necessary to freeze the Arab revolution at a particular point in order to make the required technological jump. In his view, to the contrary, the Arabs should emulate the Vietnamese fighters who are able to solve

> the difficult equation of defusing the American scientific and technological superiority and neutralizing it to their advantage with an analogous scientific mind that attained – by means of their popular political, fighting, and military experiences – a level of scientific progress in planning, inventing, organizing, and precision in implementation that no popular revolution had achieved before.

If the Arab revolution has been unable until now to achieve the conditions for its victory, Dr. al-Azm believes that its regimes and movements are responsible in the first degree for the fact of underdevelopment, and that they have to bear the consequences.

The Position of the Intellectuals

What Dr. al-Azm says includes much truth. We do not demand of the obsolete reactionary regimes that they transform the fragmented underdeveloped Arab societies to an Arab society that bears the characteristics of the age and the signs of its progress. We do expect progressive and revolutionary movements and regimes to achieve these goals. However, precision and objectivity demand of us that we identify the obstacles that make it hard for the Arab revolution to modernize Arab society. One of the primary obstacles is the stand taken by the Arab intellectuals and "technocrats" concerning the revolution and the issue of social transformation in the Arab nation.

In fact, a large segment of Arab intellectuals opposes the Arab revolution and obstructs its path for a variety of reasons and goals. Some of them are hostile to the revolution because they come from the classes that are harmed by the social transformations necessary to grow and "modernize." There is no doubt that these make up a large segment of the Arab intellectuals. For culture and science were until recently restricted to our leisure classes. This applies in a special manner to university education and the institutes of applied science in the universities like medicine, engineering, and others. Just as it applies in a more precise form to those who were granted the opportunity to complete their higher education abroad because of their social circumstances.

The overwhelming majority of these entirely take the side of the reactionary regimes and classes in the Arab nation. Consequently, they exploit their scientific and cultural superiority to strike a blow at the revolution and bring it to its final ruin.

Relieving the Conscience

This does not mean that every intellectual whose origins are in the working class is necessarily an ally of the revolution or one of its leading activists. Many of these try with every means to jump above their social origins, appealing to their knowledge to create a place for them among the ruling reactionaries in the Arab nation.

Their hostility against the revolution sometimes becomes more intense and sharper than the hostility of the bourgeoisie and feudalists. This stems from their desire to "relieve their conscience" of the suspicion that their social origin casts on them. All their ambition lies in gaining the life of luxury and pleasure in exchange for offering limited scientific services to the reactionary Arab rulers. After that, led the flood come.

The spread of this kind of Arab intellectual and the damage it does to the revolution is obvious and true. However, we need to direct our attention to this phenomenon if we desire a complete, objective assessment of the state of the Arab nation lest we draw imprecise conclusions.

It behooves us here to ask: Do you know how many Arab intellectuals and scientists would obey the call of revolution if it called them to renounce the high, comfortable life and join the ranks of the fighters for the sake of building a better life in our Arab societies, just as happened in China and some of the developing countries? In the opinion of the majority, only a small minority – among them Dr. al-Azm – would follow this call, most not.

Middle-roadism is the Primary Cause

Dr. al-Azm, since he disregards the question of the position of Arab intellectuals towards the Arab revolution, finds the cause of the stumbling of the Arab progressive regimes and their inability to transform Arab society to a contemporary society in the middle-roadism of their revolution and how it oscillates between offering decisive solutions to problems of the Arab and calling a truce with corrupt reality. This judgment, no doubt, contains much truth too. However, Dr. al-Azm sometimes chooses the wrong examples to prove his views. For example, he believes the discussion of whether there can be an Arab application of socialism is one of the manifestations of middle-roadism, as is the pursuing of a policy of non-alignment.

It is perhaps worth mentioning that ignoring the totality of the factors peculiar to the socialist application in the Arab nation leads to the disregarding of an important reality: the presumed relation between the socialist revolution and the revolution for unity in a nation fragmented into 14 countries. The socialist struggle in a country with finished national borders like Great Britain and France, for example, differs from the socialist struggle in a fragmented country like the Arab nation. If we believe principally in the nationalist truth.

Neutrality for Whom?

The other example that Dr. al-Azm adduces as evidence for the middle-roadism of the Arab revolution is its foreign policy, which has taken the way of "positive neutrality" and "non-alignment."

This view would be correct if the policy of "non-alignment" meant that we considered ourselves not to be in a position of open hostility to American imperialism, and if we considered ourselves not to be a part of the revolution of exploited peoples against the Western monopolists. However, this view misses the mark if it leads to a conclusion that calls for the necessity of abandoning the independence of the Arab Revolution as a condition of the renouncing of middle-roadism and the oscillation between revolutionary resolve and the non-revolutionary laxity in our foreign policy.

Cuba, in fact, is not neutral in its hostility to imperialism, but it, despite this, reserves the right to criticize all of the socialist countries publicly without detracting from its revolutionary character or its firmness in the face of American colonialism.

The resolute stance of Cuba towards American imperialism is what leads it most of the time to dissent from the strategy of "peaceful coexistence" maintained by the greater part of the communist parties in the world – at their head, the Soviet communist party. Perhaps this applies to us to a great extent, for if we were to consent to abandoning the independence of the Arab revolution, its many consequences would fall more under the articles of agreement between the great powers than it would fall under the achieving of the goals of the Arab revolution.

Accomplishments and Classes

In the eyes of Dr. al-Azm, the middle-roadism of the Arab revolution appears too in the nature of its internal accomplishments and the classes and forces that have led it until now. Here the author touches on the chief cause of the weakness of the Arab revolution, proclaiming his faith that the salvation of the Arabs from the depths to which they have fallen is entrusted to the eruption of

> new revolutionary powers from an Arab nation whose leadership becomes finally committed to the causes of the great majority of the individual members of the Arab people, that is, the causes of the toiling masses and the interests of the working classes...because only this kind of leadership will be capable of carrying the burdens of transforming the deeds of the fedayeen into a real popular war of liberation in which the mobilized masses participate effectively. (p. 166)

What distinguishes the book *Self-Criticism after the Defeat* finally is the inflection of sincerity and frankness that emerges from each of its chapters. Whether the reader agrees with what is said in the book in part or as a whole, he will inevitably find that it differs greatly from the arts of scoffing or lauding that have encountered wide circulation in the marketplace of political struggle in the Arab countries. On that basis, Dr. al-Azm has fulfilled his promise to his readers and appraisers and offered a book printed with the spirit of scientific fairness and, consequently, contributed to giving back to criticism its real meaning: "the precise analysis that identifies weak spots, sources of helplessness, and influences that have lead to the existence of faults and shortcomings." (p. 7)

III

Self-Criticism after the Defeat

JAMAL AL-SHARQAWI

Al-Katib [*The Writer*] **magazine, Cairo, issue 94, January 1969,**
Arab Affairs

Since the Six Day War, the dialogue with the self has spread
throughout every corner of the Arab world, in a tireless attempt to
explain what happened and deduce the consequences in order to
seek guidance on what will occur. It has become clear now that this
dialogue has divided into two basic currents and orientations, each
of them viewing the events from a particular angle, and drawing
from them what fits that angle.

The first direction was quicker in expressing itself since it did not
need to undergo any kind of struggle with itself during the dialogue.
Indeed, it came with a preconceived position: it was hostile to the
Arab national struggle at every level, and took the side of colonialism and advocated its interests constantly. The war had hardly
occurred, and the military defeat taken place, when its followers
began to wrap themselves in "rationality," "realism," foreknowledge
of the consequences, mouthing expressions of Schadenfreude and
spreading despair everywhere and over every attempt that might
enable the Arabs to eliminate the defeat and its traces, and moreover, over any hope in defeating colonialism and its agent Israel.

One of the most prominent attempts of this defeatist orientation to express itself is in an article that the Beirut newspaper
Al-Hayat (one of the newspapers of the tripartite pact) published
under the title "The Promise of the War and the Requirements of
the War." This article was republished by the Tunisian newspaper

Al-'Amal, the voice of the ruling party in Tunis, on September 8, 1968, which strove to introduce it in the following terms, which themselves are telling:

> In the series of articles by independent writers that we are reviewing along with the noble reader on the circumstances of the eastern wing of the Arab World, they are trying to analyze current data by the light of reason, appealing to history and its eternal verities!

The article mentioned emphasizes that it is entirely impossible for the Arabs to defeat Israel, for reasons that appear, from its point of view, essential and unchangeable. Among them are the following:

1) We Arabs have not known a real war for hundreds of years, for while the Arabs were soldiers with the Mamlukes and then with the Ottomans, we did not have a state with which to wage war, and so we have not formed military traditions and lack experience with armies and how to handle the enemy, whether the battle ends in victory or defeat.
2) Ignorance cannot fight a war with knowledge. The eastern Arab countries, across which, except for Lebanon, the proportion of illiterates varies from 64 to 95 percent according to UNESCO statistics, is not able to overcome an educated country that has banished illiteracy – that is, Israel.
3) Peoples who suffer from psychological complexes, and intellectual obstacles and blockages that close their minds in the face of modern civilization are not able to confront a rational western society.

Its conclusion is that there is no use, and that the Arabs should surrender to the unavoidable defeat, that is, acquiesce to the Zionist and colonialist domination!

* * *

In contrast to this, a second orientation has begun to ripen and crystallize. It is a revolutionary orientation that starts from a commitment that does not deviate from the socialist and nationalist Arab revolution. It has a deep faith in the people and the tremendous powers within them. It has an unlimited trust in a victorious future for the just struggle of the nation...regardless of the defeats and setbacks, and no matter how pale and full of dark clouds the present appears.

This orientation does not emanate from a pre-conceived position, as the client defeatist orientation does. For it emerges by means of bitter and violent struggle with the self, and through the difficult operation of discriminating between what is negative and what is positive, what is essential and what is accidental...and what is possible and what is impossible.

We are not exaggerating when we state that the best of those who express this revolutionary orientation with clarity and precision is Dr. Sadik Jalal al-Azm in the worthy study that he completed in August 1968 in Beirut, and that Dar al-Tali'ah published in the series "The Arab Thinkers."

Since the magazine does not allow a comprehensive review of this study, we will limit ourselves to summarizing some of what it includes, without entailing any diminution of the value of the remainder.

Dr. al-Azm commences in his study with the hope that

> enlightened Arab thinking will have surpassed the stage in which criticism is considered merely the activity of disparagement or the unending enumeration of defects, faults, and shortcomings. In other words, that it will have achieved a stage capable of considering criticism as the precise analysis that identifies weak spots, sources of helplessness, and influences that lead to the presence of these faults and shortcomings. Every criticism undertaken with this understanding is bound to be purposive in its unfolding and positive in its outcome, regardless of how negative and harsh it may appear at first sight. (p. 7)

The first issue that he treats is the different methods with which many wiggle out of responsibility for the defeat and cast responsibility either on others or on circumstances external to their will or greater than them. He discusses and refutes these methods with the purpose of exposing any step towards diminishing responsibility for the Arab condition by fabricating delusions, self-deception, and searching for false pretexts...considering that as a failure to recognize the truth of the illness, and thus failing to make a sound diagnosis that offers the chance for treatment and the prevention of a reoccurrence.

1) One of these methods is the describing of the June War with Israel as an aggression, and an aggression relying on an element of double-cross and surprise. The author of the study calls for the investigation and testing of these descriptions and their application to reality, for while the establishment of Israel was originally an aggression against Arab lands and Palestinian sovereignty, this aggression has existed for a long time and has not changed its nature because Israel still exists. The Arabs have been in a state of constant war with Israel since 1948, and this state also has not changed because its causes are still with us.

What is shocking is that we repeat this day and night, and consider it an issue that is impervious to any kind of negotiation. However, then, "can there be, in truth, something by the name of 'aggression' when we consider ourselves to be in a constant state of war with the other side?" (p. 27)

According to the author, the application of the description "aggression" to the June War is part of an attempt to hide a real shortcoming that the existing condition of the war required, and an attempt to hide this defect by saying that Israel made an aggression against us, as if it were only natural to expect from it good neighborliness and fair dealings.

It does not diminish the error to trace the source of the victory the enemy gained in the first hours to a "double-cross" that rested on surprise. In the view of the writer, this deluded picture of the war ignores the simplest principles of modern war, and that is its reliance on surprise attack. Moreover, we proclaimed constantly that we were turning our efforts towards the greatest goal, the battle for liberation, and therefore it is not appropriate for us to be surprised by a battle that we were constantly preparing for.

Therefore, excusing the defeat through the surprise attack of the enemy appears a frivolous evasion of all the commitments that we announced earlier, as it also means the Arabs entered the war with a chivalric conception of war still dominating their minds and reactions. There is nothing more indicative of this than the expressions, judgments, and values that we heard in our broadcasts and repeated in our newspapers, and our sayings about the clinking of swords, attack and retreat, "strings of horses," and the personal tribal conceptions of the meaning of courage, the defiance of death, honor, zeal, deception, baseness, and direct face-to-face confrontation in battle.

2) Among these methods is also the removal of responsibility as a whole and in part and casting it onto colonialism. Dr. al-Azm asks if the Arabs were not fully aware that Israel had close organic ties with the colonialists? And was the United States not clear, leaving no room for doubt, about its intentions towards the Arabs and the extent of its readiness to support and maintain Israel? How can you blame the wolf for its behaving like a wolf?

The author proceeds after that to a dangerous delusion, that there is a distinction between "the power of Israel in itself" and the powers it draws from others, which is the basis for the idea that the Arabs would with certainty overpower Israel if they confronted its capacity alone.

This is a dubious distinction, because, in the end, the powers of Israel in itself are everything that it is able to throw into the battle, whether from inside Israel or whatever assistance is advanced from outside.

However, the most dangerous element in this distinction is that it disregards from a practical position the characterization that is repeated every day in every corner of the Arab nation, that Israel is nothing but a colonialist base. How can we regard a base as if it were a, standing on its own legs, in isolation from the colonialism that created it, and treat it as if it were the starting point of its domination, its projects, and its conspiracies? It is, in the end, a distinction that forms part of a deluded hope that colonialism will one day renounce Israel for us, leaving it to its own strength, so that we confront it and triumph over it!

3) Among the mistaken ideas about the causes of the defeat is the notion that if Cairo had taken the initiative and begun the battle,

the situation would be reversed and the Arabs would have triumphed. The basic error in this way of thinking is that it ignores the objective circumstances that led to the defeat. It, rather, attributes the defeat to an accident or an error in estimation. This is also a delusion, one that attempts to convince us that we were capable of victory if we had not been delayed. However, it neglects that we knew that Israel would take the initiative, and that we knew well when it would take the initiative, and how. Despite this, we were not ready for all of that or even less than that. Here lies the essential cause and not in the delay and lack of initiative.

4) There is also a very simple and widespread explanation that attributes the Arab defeats to Israel to international Zionist domination over the whole world.

Dr. Jalal al-Azm gives this topic a very significant treatment, and it begins like this:

> Of the terrible errors that the Arabs have fallen into as far as their cause is concerned, the first is the extreme underestimation of the capacity of the enemy. The second terrible error that the Arab appraisal of Zionism and its power has fallen into is the exaggeration of its power and influence to the extent of ascribing it overwhelming mythical powers that make it the mistress of capitalism, socialism, and the course of history at the same time. (p. 54, 55)

Then the author uncovers the meaning of this falling into error, which he attributes to the desire to rationalize the defeat and blame it on a force outside of our will and larger than us. (For how can we blame ourselves if we are not able to answer the Zionist challenge if we are confronting a power that dominates the life and fate of both the capitalist bloc and communist bloc at the least.) Then he offers two examples of this exaggeration of the power of the enemy.

The first example is the sillier. Its advocates have recourse to the *Protocol of the Elders of Zion* to prove that the Jews have gained total domination by means of a hellish world conspiracy over the course of modern history:

According to this superstitious logic, the Elders of Zion gather together at least once every century where they carry out discussions and studies in order to compose their frightening secret plan to enslave the world. The creators of this "theory" of historical explanation assure us that the course of history proceeds, without the least doubt, according to the plans of the conspiracy, not deviating an inch because of the cleverness of the Jewish leaders and their excessive intelligence and unlimited influence, making them masters of planning and implementation for a century at a time with an unimaginable efficiency. (p. 54)

As for the second example, it inclines towards the reasonable, since it attributes the power of the Jews and Zionists to the dominance of the Jews over the American economy and from there to hegemony over the major capitalist country, directing its policies in accordance with the interests of Israel.

In his discussion of these issues, the author returns to the book, *Al-Aqaliyyat al-Yehudiah f'il Wilayat al-Mutihadat al-Amrikiyah* [*The Jewish Minority in the United States of America*], by Mustafa 'Abd al-'Aziz, published by the PLO Research Center in 1968. This makes clear from the facts mentioned that:

Jewish interests only dominate some limited regions of the middle sectors of the American economy, and thus fall short of controlling general economic activity in the country. The following are some examples of economic areas that submit to the influence of the Jews, either partly or as a whole: the manufacture of men's and women's apparel almost as a whole; the fur industry; fashion, design, and cosmetics; wholesale and retail trade in some merchandise types; jewelry; the grocery business; spirits, import and export; the film industry and the media in general, including publishing houses. Just as the Jews enjoy a strong influence as stockbrokers (especially in New York) and in professional areas such as law, medicine, dentistry, and university teaching. (p. 62)

This is nothing to be scoffed at; however, we should not exaggerate its weight:

> all of these economic sectors falling under Jewish control are nothing but drops in the sea in comparison to the basic sectors that form the sensitive nerve of the American economy, where we find the source of real political power. Let us include some examples of the companies that American society thrives with or fades with: Standard Oil and the other oil companies; Dupont; large steel companies from U.S. Steel (the largest) to Bethlehem Steel (the sixth in size); in the area of money transfers and banks, Bank of America, Chase Manhattan Bank, First National City Bank; the famous large airline companies; the main automobile manufacturers; the big advertising companies; agribusiness...There is not the slightest doubt that the Jews lack influence in this main sector – they are not allowed to approach it at all, and thus cannot dominate it.

The author here states that the reason for this has its source in the racial character of American society:

> The group with hegemony in the American economy is the "White Protestants," as they are called in the United States, or WASPs, the acronym for White Anglo-Saxon Protestants. However you look, you will not find the Jews (or even Catholics) having any real power or influence worth mentioning in these sensitive centers or leadership in any of the institutions or companies that I have cited.

Mustafa 'Abd al-'Aziz points to the scarcity of Jews working in banks, saying:

> It appears that in 45 of these banks, there is not a single Jewish employee at the senior level. In four of them, there is only one Jew at the senior level. In one bank there are four Jews in the higher positions, and only 32 Jews out of a total of the 3,438 employees found in middle management.

Dr. al-Azm infers from this:

> The prevalence of the delusion of total Jewish domination of the American economy and its wide circulation among Arab citizens is a result, at best, of ignorance of American economic conditions and facts, and of our wish to adopt a quick and simple explanation for American behavior towards the Palestinian cause. At worst, it is a deliberate attempt to clear non-Jewish America (in other words, the actual America with its extensive economy, interests, colonialism, etc.) from responsibility for hostile actions against the Arab nation and for active participation in the driving out of the Palestinian Arab people. (p. 67)

Another important matter that the study of Dr. al-Azm investigates is the matter of the necessity of adopting the most modern science and technology as a way to develop Arab society and face the challenges of colonialism and Zionism.

The study proposes this question on a number of bases of considerable value:

1) The June defeat would not be truly necessary to realize the importance of science and technology if we did not regard modern science as one of the slogans tossed around without realizing what scientific rationality means at the level of daily practice and cumulative, continuous, concrete application.

2) No two Arabs differ about the necessity of adopting science and technology. The problem is what happens after the discussion of the necessity. We ought not to remain at the level of abstraction, generality, and universality, but instead we ought to enter into the details, criticize, and propose precise practical solutions.

3) Adopting the deep development of society by means of science and technology does not ever mean the call for delaying the direct struggle against the occupation or the delaying of the battle for liberation with the Zionists until we overcome Arab technological and scientific backwardness. For "in reality, we are with those who believe that the struggle for a strong, scientific, and modern socialist Arab society is tightly,

directly, and organically bound with the Arab battle against the Zionists and its imperialist supporters." (p. 102)

The author of the study defines his position concerning the intellectual battle revolving around this topic among different social forces in these words:

> Some of the commentators on the Arab conditions after the defeat (and especially the progressives among them) seem to presume that a discussion of the defeat from the point of view of the prevailing scientific level in some particular Arab countries, for example, and on the basis of the question of modernity and the renewal of the means of production and social relationships in their comprehensive meanings is nothing but flight from the confrontation of the occupation and the battle for liberation by means of a popular war of liberation. Their evidence is the current fact that raising the level of the Arab nation in terms of science and production and its transformation to a modern society, etc. forms a long process absorbing generations, while the present occupation of Arab land cannot endure such a delay.

However, he also realizes:

> The liberal Arab circles calling for a modern Arab society want to make from the call for the triumph over under-development a substitute for the only Arab response with guaranteed results to the expansionist Zionist presence on Arab lands, namely, a popular war of liberation.

What is the correct position?

> The basic error in this pattern of thinking is stating the case in such a way as to create an apparent conflict between the striving of the nation and its revolutionary leadership in hope of overcoming underdevelopment and advancing towards a modern society, on the one hand, and the method of the popular war of liberation (with what it requires in

the way of a mobilization and organization of the popular masses) in confronting the enemy, on the other hand. The incompatibility between these two goals is nothing but a delusion, since the great masters of the popular war of liberation in this century have never passed up an opportunity to insist – at the level of theory and practice – that the consequences of a war of liberation are the shaking of the traditional fabric of social life and the striking at its various indifferent, lazy, and sluggish relationships, customs, and values, which are inimical and obstructive to the process of modernization itself. That is, the war of liberation – in the view of its leaders and their experiences – facilitates the process of modernization, accelerates it in an unparalleled manner, and radically levels the path to the building of a modern, scientifically socialist society after the end of the war. The significance of the popular war of liberation is not latent in only its "negative" consequences, like the driving out of the occupation and the emancipation from the hegemony of the colonizer entirely, but also in its positive consequences, since the direct or indirect participation of the individual in the resistance or popular military efforts leads by necessity to the widening of that individual's horizons so that he comprehends the existence of his country and nation, not merely that of his tribe and family. It also creates in the individual a sense of his integral importance in the national effort and the building of the nation, and strengthens in him the values of discipline, reliability, and the appreciation of work, time, and the rest of the general and necessary considerations for the process of modernization and building a modern socialist state. (p. 103, 104)

Dr. al-Azm brings to mind the aspects of backwardness in the realm of technology in order to make clear the following:

- From the ocean to the gulf, there is only one Arab state that has undertaken an organized plan to invest in scientific research, the United Arab Republic.

- With its oil and its hundred million citizens, the Arab nation does not contain one institute that grants a scientific degree in electronics.
- According to the study of Dr. Wasfi Hijab (*Al-Fikr al-'Arabiya fi Mi'at Sannah* [in *Arabic Thought in One Hundred Years*], Publications of the Centenary, American University of Beirut, 1967), of the 1,500 scientific journals cited, there is found only one Arabic-language journal, which is *The Journal of the United Arab Republic for Chemistry*, and Arab scientists published almost one thousand studies in international scientific journals in the year 1965, nine-tenths of the publications being from the United Arab Republic and the greater portion of the remaining tenth being published by scientists at the American University of Beirut. As for the rest of the Arab nation, in regards to scientific production it is a barren and sterile desert. Dr. Hijab concludes from this that "if we take into consideration that the inhabitants of the Arab world are almost three percent of the world population and that scientific production in 1965 was almost one million scientific papers, then the Arab world contributed only three percent of its share relative to its population."

The author also offers a number of prominent models of how to overcome scientific backwardness.

The Chinese government waited only one month after the triumph of the revolution in 1949 to establish a Chinese Academy for the Sciences, then directed an invitation to Chinese scientists working in foreign universities to join it. These formed a nucleus of modern scientific revival whose effects appeared in the exploding of a Chinese hydrogen bomb before France, which has a deep industrial and scientific tradition.

In the Soviet Union, Stalin's call in 1931 that "we must study technology and gain complete mastery over science, etc." had clear effects, which prompted the American magazine *Time* to mention in 1957 in the course of criticizing some aspects of scientific life in the United States that Soviet universities and institutes graduated twice as many engineers as those in the United States per year, and that the Soviet government was bestowing money almost without counting to develop both theoretical and applied scientific research because it considers it a necessary condition for its increasing economic growth, military and political power, and international status.

He introduces us to the curious comparison between our condition and the similar condition of the United States of America – despite the ample difference. He points out the shock that befell the United States in the winter of 1957 when the Soviet Union launched its first satellite, an extraordinary achievement that the United States had been unable to attain at that time.

What was the American reaction (always remember that we are discussing America) to this setback? The experts demanded a re-evaluation of all their educational programs at every level, from primary schools to the largest laboratories for nuclear research, in order to identify their weak spots and strengthen them. An example is the criticisms one of the senior experts made concerning the secondary educational programs: "the programs for mathematics taught in our secondary institutions are anachronistic since the concepts of mathematics and physics that prevail are those that prevailed in the nineteenth century, just as they are no longer able to tie together the information taught with the science of mathematics as an integrated unit." The famous nuclear scientist Edward Teller (the maker of the world's first hydrogen bomb) warned the Americans of the consequences of not taking scientific research seriously for overcoming the setback, stating that "the Russians regard science as if it were their religion, and they regard their scientists with the utmost degree of respect," pointing out the deteriorating situation of American scientists and teachers.

Dr. al-Azm believes that in order to remedy our scientific and technological underdevelopment and profit from the experience of others, we must pursue these ends:

a) The accelerating of the establishment of expert Arab institutes in strategic studies, electronics, the applied sciences, petrochemical engineering, etc.;

b) The re-evaluation of all our educational programs at every stage, with the goal of their development according to the most modern methods;

c) An invitation to all Arab scientists who work in foreign scientific institutes, universities, and centers to return to the nation, with the provision of incentives and conditions that would encourage and suit them. These would attract them and promote their success. The first thing would be to study the conditions that led them to their emigration, including what would prevent this emigration;

d) The profiting from the experiences of preparing, polishing, and developing young talents, one of the pioneers of which is the Soviet Union. Continuing the long tradition of devoting special institutes to children with extraordinary artistic talents (music, ballet, etc.), the Soviet government applied this tradition to male and female students who had superior abilities in mathematics, physics, and natural sciences, teaching typical secondary school curricula to primary school students in order to produce the greatest possible number of outstanding scientists in the shortest possible time, and without wasting the time of these young geniuses in the usual school drudgery. The special curricula in mathematics include, for example, topics that are not typically taught except at the university level, like analytical geometry, theoretical mechanics, applications of mathematics to physics, differential calculus, etc. Therefore, the universities supervise the composition of these special curricula.

This experiment has had great success, which has induced Mr. Lewis Strauss, the president of the Atomic Energy Commission in the United States, to say in 1957:

> I can learn of no public high school in our country where a student obtains so thorough a preparation in science and mathematics, even if he seeks it – even if he should be a potential Einstein.

Dr. Sadik Jalal al-Azm's study is considered correctly as one of the exemplary studies in deep and serious research of the causes of the defeat. It is at the same time a brilliant example of the positive constructive critique that aims to profit from understanding the errors in order to direct the movement of society towards progress. It is one of the flashes of contemporary Arab conscience and a prominent sign on the path of our revolutionary consciousness.